W9-CFC-273

ESTONIA
at a Glance

 oomen

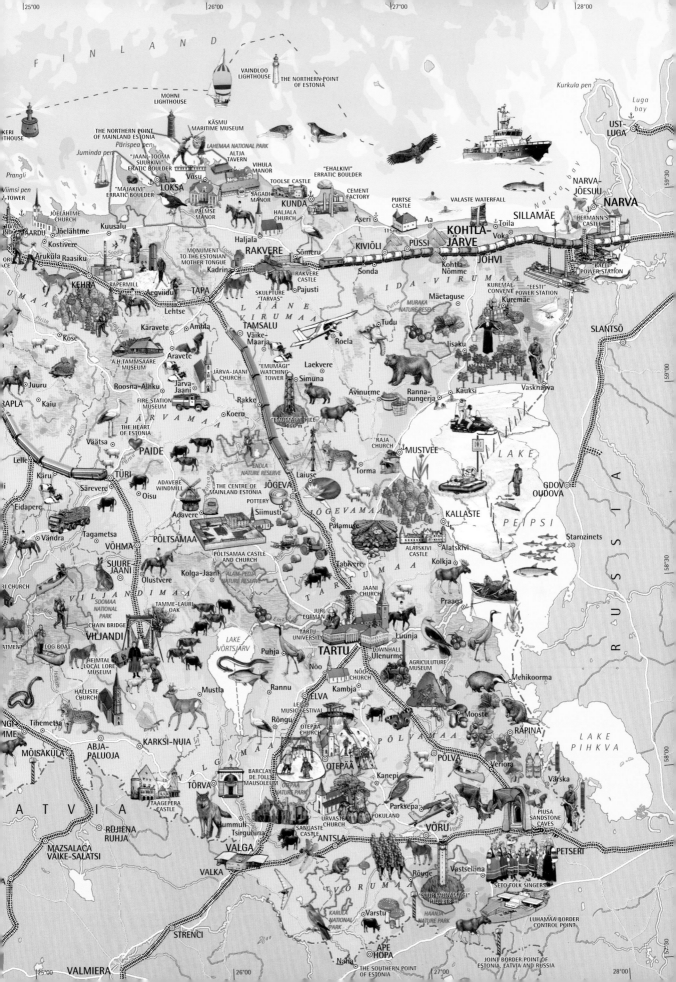

Contributors
Andres Tõnisson,
Ado Keskpaik,
Hanna Miller
English translator
Mart Aru
Photographers
Jarek Jõepera, Toomas Tuul, Arne Ader,
Lembit Michelson, Meelis Lokk, Malev Toom,
Toomas Volmer, Ain Avik, Ülo Josing, Jüri Pere,
Marko Mumm, Andres Tüür, Raivo Tiikmaa,
Ivo Musting, Jaak Neljandik, Heiko Kruusi,
Gunnar Fardelin /RV Pildipank/.
Tiit Leito, Arvo Tingas, Toomas Kokovkin,
Tiit Kitkas, Mart Mõniste/www.fotokogu.com/,
Saaremaa Museum archive
Map
AS Regio. ©Regio 2006, www.regio.ee
Designer
Sirje Tooma

© Oomen Publishers 2006

All rights reserved. No part of this publication may be
reproduced, stored in a retrieval system, or transmitted in any
form or by any means, electronic, mechanical, photocopying,
recording or otherwise, without the prior written permission of
the copyright owner

oomen@oomen.ee

www.oomen.ee

Endla 3 / 2155
10122 Tallinn
Estonia

ISBN-10 9985-9697-0-7 (soft cover)
ISBN-13 978-9985-9697-0-0 (soft cover)

ISBN-10 9985-9697-1-5 (hard cover)
ISBN-13 978-9985-9697-1-7 (hard cover)

HISTORY
NATURE
PRINCIPAL CITIES
PLACES OF
INTEREST
300
COLOUR
PHOTOGRAPHS
& MAP

ESTONIA
at a Glance

THE COUNTRY AND THE PEOPLE

TALLINN

The Country and the People

General

With a population of just 1.35 million in 2005, Estonia is one of the smallest countries in Europe. It is small also in territory, 45,200 square kilometres, but still larger than Denmark, Switzerland or the Netherlands.

More than two thirds, 69 percent of the population live in towns and 31 per cent in rural areas. The biggest cities are Tallinn, the capital of Estonia (397,000 inhabitants), the university town of Tartu (101,000), the industrial cities of Narva (68,000) and Kohtla-Järve (47,000) and the seaside resort of Pärnu (45,000). The density of population is low – an average of 31 inhabitants per square kilometre, and only 10 inhabitants per square kilometre in the countryside.

Estonian-speakers make up 68 per cent, Russian-speakers 26 per cent and other nationalities 6 per cent of the population. Non-Estonian speakers mainly live in Tallinn and in the northeast of the country.

The main source of livelihood is services (61 per cent), with 32 per cent employed in industry and only 6 per cent in agriculture and fishery.

Estonia is a parliamentary republic.

The country belongs to the European Union since 2004.

The beach in Pärnu, Estonia's summer capital ▷
Bicycle rally in Tartu ▷
Nature trail through bogland ▷

△ **Many Estonian bogs have plank walks for the convenience of hikers**

Nature

Estonia is situated on the eastern coast of the Baltic Sea at the edge of the East-European Plain. Lakes Peipsi and Pskov, together forming the fourth biggest freshwater body in Europe, constitute the natural boundary between Estonia and Russia. In the north the Gulf of Finland separates Estonia from Finland and in the west the closest neighbour is Sweden across the Baltic Sea. Most of the southern border between Estonia and Latvia passes through extensive forested areas. There are 1,500 islands and islets, 11 of them inhabited, the largest of them being Saaremaa and Hiiumaa.

Estonia has traces of surface features dating back to before the last Ice Age. The most striking of them is the Baltic Clint, which stretches 1,200 kilometres from Sweden's Öland Island to Lake Ladoga in Russia. In some places along the northern shore the limestone bluff, the most spectacular natural monument in Estonia, rises to nearly 60 meters above sea level. The country's largely level relief was mainly shaped by the Ice Age, which ended in these parts in about 10,000 B C. The rolling landscape in the south of the country as well as the loaf-like drumlins of central Estonia principally consist of deposits left behind by continental ice. Suur-Munamägi, the highest point in the Baltic countries, rising 318 metres above sea level, lies in the Haanja Uplands in the southeast.

Immediately after the Ice Age, the low-lying areas of northern and western Estonia were still flooded and so the relief of that area is younger still. Some of the most conspicuous signs of the Ice Age are erratic boulders carried to their present location by continental ice from Scandinavia and Finland. Some of them are the size of small houses.

Estonia boasts relatively numerous areas that are in a pristine or near pristine state. The large wetland regions and swampy forests, the combined result of level relief and wet climate, were not taken into intensive economic use even in the mid-20th century when the respective pressure was the highest. One fifth of the Estonian land area is wetlands and 40 per cent is forested. The extensive woodlands are the habitat of several species of animals and birds that have practically become extinct elsewhere in Europe. We could mention the white-tailed eagle, the brown bear, the lynx, the wolf, the beaver etc. The elk, the wild boar and the roe deer are ordinary game animals in Estonia.

Considering its small territory the landscape in Estonia is quite varied. The narrow North-Estonian coastal lowland below the bluff is indented with numerous small bays. Small characteristic fishing villages and holiday settlements lie between the sea and the pinewoods. South of the line of the bluff the land is higher but level, turned into fields or

◁ **Icebound Jägala Falls**

△ One of Estonia's thousand picture-book lakes

covered with forests. In the northeast, oil shale mining and processing has created large man-made surface features. These include huge waste and ash heaps, strip mines and fly-ash fields. Western Estonia and the vicinity of Lakes Võrtsjärv and Peipsi have some of the biggest wetlands in the country. In the islands and the western part of the mainland the population is concentrated along the coastline. The old villages there feature more traditional farm building than elsewhere. The best arable lands are inland, around Rakvere, Paide, Jõgeva and Viljandi, where the soil is richer and fields larger. In the southeastern uplands picturesque woods on rounded hills alternate with lakes, small patches of field and isolated farmsteads.

Estonia has several national parks, landscape reserves and numerous nature parks that make up a total of nearly 15 per cent of the country's territory. These areas are suitable for hiking, listening to the sounds of nature and watching animals and birds either independently or in the company of experienced guides.

◁ Hilly landscape in southern Estonia
◁ Jaani-Tooma Suurkivi, deposited where it stands by continental ice

History

People settled in the territory of present-day Estonia after the continental ice retrea-ted. The oldest traces of human settlement found until the present date back to the 9th millennium B C. Although opinions differ concerning the ethnic background of the oldest inhabitants, scientists do agree that tribes speaking a Finno-Ugric language – ancestors of present-day Estonians – lived in this land at least three thousand years before Christ. So the Estonians can be considered to be one of the oldest stationery peoples in Europe.

By the early 13th century the Estonian tribes, subsisting mainly on agriculture, had remained some of the last pagans in Europe between two Christian civilizations – the Catholics of the West and the Orthodox Christians of the East. At the beginning of the 13th century mostly German, but also Danish, crusaders conquered the lands of the Estonians and other tribes settling the eastern shores of the Baltic Sea and turned the subjugated peoples to Christianity, with the Pope's blessing.

The area of present-day Estonia and Latvia where the crusaders established their feudal states in the 13th–16th centuries and introduced European social relations has become known as Old Livonia. Estonian chiefs and wealthy Estonians either fell in the fighting or were assimilated with the upper layer of foreigners. In the period from the 13th to the 20th centuries the history of present-day Estonia was shaped by different foreign powers, but it was the Baltic-German nobility, formed of the crusaders' descendents, that remained the most influential social stratum both economically and politically through the centuries. The indigenous people, who called themselves *maarahvas*, the people of the land, were reduced to the status of peasantry after the subjugation and languished in serfdom. They constituted the lowest strata of the population also in the cities the conquerors had built and where the leading role belonged to German-born merchants and craftsmen. Several Estonian cities were members of the Hanseatic League, a union of trading cities along the Baltic Sea coasts, with Lübeck in Germany as its mother city. German municipal law (charters of Lübeck or Riga) was applied in the cities. Tallinn (then known as Reval), Narva and Tartu (Dorpat), hubs of transit trade with Russia, were among the most important hanseatic cities in Estonian lands. At the end of the period, ideas of reformation arrived in Estonia in the 1520s and the Lutheran church was finally established around the middle of the century.

Old Livonia ceased to exist as a result of the Livonian War (1558–1583), as well as later wars between Russia, Sweden, Denmark and Poland-Lithuania. In 1561 the nobility of the present northern Estonia and the city of Tallinn swore allegiance to Sweden. In the following centuries that area was called Estland. Areas further south that came to be referred to as Liefland gave themselves under the protection of Poland-Lithuania, but by 1645 the whole of Estonia was under Swedish rule. The provinces on the eastern shore of the Baltic were important for Sweden as a granary as well as a trade route to Russia. Narva was a bridgehead of particular importance on the transit route, and Sweden even considered turning it into its eastern capital where the king would reside every fourth year. King Gustavus II Adolphus founded the country's first university in Tartu in 1632. Establishment of peasant schools also began in the Swedish period. The situation of the peasantry was somewhat alleviated by the restitution of manors, but the old status system remained in force even under the Swedes.

The Great Northern War that broke out in 1700, with Poland, Russia, Saxony and Denmark making up the anti-Swedish coalition, brought Estonia into the composition of the Russian empire for more than two hundred years. The social relations

△ Ruins of the Vastseliina Order Castle
△ Prehistoric Soontagana stronghold in Pärnu County
△ Koluvere Castle, Lääne County
△ Restored entrance to the prehistoric Varbola stronghold

established in the Baltic provinces since the Middle Ages remained unchanged under the Russian rule. It was important for the Russian tsars to uphold the loyalty of the ruling strata. Besides, the Russian tsars, wishing to make Russia more European, regarded the Baltic provinces as an example to other parts of the country. The Baltic-German nobility gained a great influence in St Petersburg, the new Russian capital built very close to Estonia – just 150 kilometres from Narva – as well as in the imperial court. A large number of world famous statesmen, soldiers, scholars and scientists emerged from among their midst. Let us here mention the biologists Karl Ernst von Baer (1792–1876) and Jakob Johann von Uexküll (1864–1944), the navigators, discoverer of the Antarctic Fabian Gottlieb von Bellingshausen (1778–1852) and leader of the first Russian expedition around the world Adam Johann von Krusenstern (1770–1846), explorer of Siberia Alexander Theodor von

▽ **Gustavus II Adolphus of Sweden,** founder of Tartu University

▽ **Karl Ernst von Baer, one of prominent** Tartu University scientists

▽ **Russian General Field Marshal** Barclay de Tolly

▽ **Friedrich Reinhold Kreutzwald,** author of the national epic

▽ **Lydia Koidula, the foremost poetess of** the national movement period

Middendorff (1815–94), polar explorer Eduard Gustav von Toll (1858–1902), commander-in-chief of the Russian army Field Marshal Barclay de Tolly (1761–1818), philosopher Hermann Alexander von Keyserling (1880–1946), writer Eduard von Keyserling (1855–1918), the geologist and explorer, honorary member of the St Petersburg Academy of Sciences Alexander Friedrich von Keyserling (1815–91), the artist, Professor of the St Petersburg Academy of Arts Carl Timoleon von Neff (1804–77) and many others.

Changes leading to the formation of a modern society gradually began in the 19th century. Serfdom was abolished in Estonia in 1816 and in the second half of the century the peasants gained the opportunity of buying their farms in perpetuity. The national movement that had encompassed the whole of Europe reached also Estonia. The Estonians began to see themselves as one nation and the national intelligentsia was gradually formed. After the example of the Finnish *Kalevala* Friedrich Reinhold Kreutzwald (1803–82) wrote the Estonian national epic *Kalevipoeg*, while Lydia Koidula (1843–86) established herself as the foremost patriotic poetess. Carl Robert Jakobson (1841–82), a radical journalist, author of schoolbooks and promoter of agriculture, played an important role in the national movement. The first Estonian-wide song festival, held in Tartu in 1969, was a prominent milestone in the consolidation of the nation. In the final decades of the 19th century industrial development promoted the growth of towns. In counterbalance to the rise in national self-awareness, the Russian tsarist government introduced policies of Russification starting with the 1880s,

making Russian the language of state administration and of tuition in nearly all schools, rescinding many privileges the Baltic-German nobility had been enjoying since they were granted to them by Peter I and increasing influence of the Russian Orthodox church. Early in the new century power in the expanding cities passed to Estonian and Russian political forces.

In the political situation established as a result of the World War and the Russian Revolution it became possible for Estonia to proclaim independence. An Estonian Salvation Committee headed by Konstantin Päts (1874–1956), later state elder and president of the country, promulgated a Manifesto of Independence on 24 February 1918. The young country had to be immediately defended in a War of Independence (1918–20) against Soviet Russia. Estonian forces headed by commander-in chief Johan Laidoner (1884–53) received support from countries of the Entente and Finland. The Republic of Estonia expropriated most of the lands that had belonged to Baltic-German landowners and abrogated all privileges of status. Estonian was made the language of tuition in all schools, including the university. The Estonian elite – politicians, public servants, industrialists, intellectuals, and a body of officers – was formed in the first period of independence that lasted until 1940.

By a secret protocol to the non-aggression pact signed between Germany and the Soviet Union (the Hitler-Stalin Pact) on the eve of World War Two Estonia along with the other Baltic nations was assigned to the Soviet sphere of influence. At Hitler's call, most Baltic-Germans left the country during a campaign called Umsiedlung in 1939. In 1940 the Soviet Union occupied and annexed Estonia and a German occupation followed later in World War Two. Both the Soviets and the Germans mobilised Estonians into their armed forces. Attempts to restore independence towards the end of the war (1944) failed and Estonia remained in the composition of the Soviet Union.

Under the Soviets the Estonians suffered from deportations, forced formation of collective farms and Soviet industrial expansion, in the course of which hundreds of thousands of people from elsewhere in the Soviet Union settled in the country. Despite a foreign ideology, the national awareness and spirit of independence survived in the Estonians thanks to the viability of their language and culture, being strong enough to launch in the late 1980s a Singing Revolution that gradually led to the restoration of national independence in 1991. Like in most other Central and East-European countries, development of democracy and a functioning market economy has permitted Estonia to consolidate its security by acceding to NATO and the European Union.

◁ **Carl Robert Jakobson, a leader of the 19th century national movement**

◁ **General Johan Laidoner – commander of the Estonian army in the War of Independence**

Pikk Hermann ▷

Places of Interest

Although Estonian nature is subdued rather that striking and extraordinary, there are still some unique natural monuments such as the limestone clint stretching parallel to the northern coast and visits to spots of beauty and nature reserves may leave a far more memorable impression than could at first be presumed, offering the joy of discovery and excitement. To visitors coming from crowded cities or densely populated parts of the world it may look surprising how much uninhabited space, peace and quiet there is in the country for everyone's free enjoyment, as access to nature is simple. From sunrise to sundown anyone may stay anywhere without asking permission, unless the owner has clearly marked the land as private – there is everyman's law in Estonia. It is also interesting that there are relatively many landscapes surviving in the natural or near-natural state. In addition to forests and bogs, the latter also include alvars – juniper stands on thin soils over a limestone bedrock (elsewhere in Europe they can only be seen on the Swedish islands of Öland and Gotland), as well as coastal meadows, water meadows and wooden meadows that stand out for the multitude of different species of plants growing in them. Natural and semi-natural landscapes are the habitat of a number of animals and birds that have become rare in Europe.

Of monuments connected with human activity remains of ancient hill forts and earthen strongholds, stone cyst graves and sacrificial stones date back to prehistoric times, when the Estonians' ancestors were still free. Most of the historical sights, however, reflect the material culture introduced by the conquerors in the period of Old Livonia (1200–1558), when stone fortresses were built in the 13th–14th centuries instead of the ancient Estonians' earthen strongholds and churches and cities were erected. In the Middle Ages there were about a hundred of stone fortresses in Estonia, but most of them were either destroyed or reduced in the 16th century Livonian War or in the course of later hostilities. Only in Tallinn, Narva, Pärnu and Kuressaare the existing fortifications were restored and strengthened even in the 17th century, but at the end of the 18th century they, too, were finally abandoned. Most of the surviving castles or their ruins are today displayed as tourist sights. Some of them, such as Kuressaare and Narva, have been turned into museums.

Consolidation of spiritual power began with the building of churches and monasteries form the 13th century onwards, where they were often put up in prehistoric Estonians' holy places – usually sacred groves. As in those times churches and monasteries also served as defence structures, it had an effect on their outward appearance. The tradition of tall steeples only widened in the 17th century. The first Orthodox churches in Estonia were built as part of the Russification campaign at the end of the 19th century. In Soviet times some churches stood empty or were used as warehouses. Later, after the re-establishment of independence, several of them have been restored to new life.

The oldest Estonian cities, where German craftsmen and merchants played the key role, grew up around medieval castles. Therefore also the structure of the towns followed the German model, with the central place belonging to the Town Hall and Town Hall Square, the church and rich citizens' and noblemen's dwelling houses. The Old City of Tallinn, which now stands in UNESCO World Heritage List, is one of the best-preserved medieval city centres in Northern Europe. As the Baltic-German supremacy became a matter of the past more than a century ago, we can see also vestiges of later periods in the present city scene in terms of planning, buildings and style. Traces of the Soviet period of half a century of massive industrialisation and urbanisation are particularly strong.

Side by side with villages and farmsteads manors still from part of the rural landscape in Estonia. Most of the manor halls extant today were built in the 18th and 19th centuries, when economic conditions were particularly favourable for Baltic-German manor lords in the Russian empire. The downfall of manors, of which there were more than a thousand in the country, began after World War I when the Estonian government carried out a land reform that stripped the manors of most of their lands. Many manors were abandoned; others were taken into use as schools or local government seats. Refurbishment and maintenance of the preserved manor halls and finding suitable uses for them is a problem until today, not to mention restoration of their once stately appearance. Those of the manor halls that today still survive to a lesser or greater degree are among key cultural sights in the given area.

Of other cultural sights museums deserve to be mentioned first. The oldest of them is the Tartu University Art Museum established in 1803. Traditional Estonian peasant culture can be seen at several open-air museums. The small Kihnu Island in the Gulf of Riga is a singular example of valuable heritage, and UNESCO has proclaimed the cultural space connected with it a masterpiece of oral and intangible heritage of humanity. It has given the same distinction to the Baltic countries' song and dance festivals, which in Estonia periodically bring together tens of thousands of performers and hundreds of thousands of public. Estonia has a fast developing health resort economy with strong traditions. Modern methods of spa therapy have long been introduced side by side with the traditional treatment by natural sea-muds. Spas in Pärnu, Kuressaare and Haapsalu provide good opportunities of rest and treatment round the year. Also Otepää, the South Estonian winter sports centre, is coming to be better and better known every year.

◁ **High sandstone bank of the Võhandu**

Tourism areas

For a better overview of its sights Estonia could be divided into four areas: Tallinn, the capital of the country, North and Northeast Estonia, West Estonia and South Estonia.

Tallinn is particularly rich in sights. Its main attraction is the historical centre, the Old Town, a well-preserved area still largely surrounded by the medieval town wall. Besides, Tallinn has a number of important museums, theatres, concert halls and sports arenas. The famous song and dance festivals and various international cultural events also take place in the city.

North and Northeast Estonia is a strip of varying width along the southern shore of the Gulf of Finland. The main sights are above all the limestone clint with its singular nature, the Lahemaa National Park, medieval castles, manor halls, the oil shale area and the border town of Narva.

West Estonia, which comprises both coastal areas of the mainland as well as offshore islands, could also be called Maritime Estonia. It has the country's main holiday resorts of Pärnu, Kuressaare and Haapsalu with their varied summer cultural programmes. Pristine nature can be seen in the Vilsandi and Matsalu National Parks. Characteristic of the region are picturesque coastal and village landscapes with juniper stands.

South Estonia roughly coincides with the area of influence of Estonia's second largest city, the university town of Tartu. That large region is characterised by versatility in terms of both landscapes and culture. It has the biggest inland water bodies – Lakes Peipsi and Võrtsjärv, large wetland areas (Soomaa National Park) as well as the changeful hilly lake-dotted landscapes of the Karula National Park and the Haanja landscape reserve. The Seto culture on the southeastern border and the Russian Old Believers' communities on Lake Peipsi clearly stand out for their local peculiarities. Numerous folk culture events take place in the area.

◁　**Skyline of Tallinn**
◁　**Northeast Estonia**
◁　**Angla windmills in Saaremaa**

▽　**Lake Pühajärv in the Otepää Highlands**

Tallinn

Tallinn, the capital of Estonia with its roughly 400,000 inhabitants, has nearly one third of the population of the whole country, and it also accounts for nearly half the gross domestic product. Being the capital, which is also a port city as well as a business, industrial and cultural centre, the pace of life in the city is fast and restless. Residents of Tallinn are probably accustomed to it, but people from other parts of Estonia on their visits to Tallinn are relieved to be leaving the city. Yet Tallinn serves as an attraction to the rest of the country and its growth at the expense of its hinterland is continuing. Tallinn is an open city. Through its seaport it has maritime links with Helsinki and Stockholm and hundreds of cruise ships visit it during the summer months. Direct flights from Tallinn connect Estonia with about a dozen European countries. Trains run from the city to St Petersburg and Moscow.

The history of Tallinn, a settlement site of prehistoric Estonians, goes back 3,500 years. For centuries the city was known as Reval after a fortress the Danes built on the citadel of Toompea following their conquest of North Estonia in 1219. The name Tallinn has been recorded in sources since 1536 (Tallyn – Danish town). The Danes have a special relationship with Tallinn. According to a legend the luck was on the Estonians' side in a heavy battle the Danes fought with them near Toompea in 1219. One of the bishops had already been killed, and King Waldemar was sending desperate prayers to the heavens… Then a red flag with a white cross fell out of the skies to the Danes, inspiring the soldiers so much that the tide turned in the Danes' favour. The Danebrog is the Danish national flag to this day, and there is a monument in Taani Kuninga aed, the Garden of the Danish King near the Megede Tower at Toompea's edge to remember the event, presumably erected where the flag once fell.

The natural preconditions that favoured the development of Tallinn into a port, trading centre and later a capital city, were a protected harbour, a hill fort that could be easily defended, fertile arable land in the vicinity and ample sources of sweet water – **Lake Ülemiste** and the River Härjapea that once flew out of it. By today the river has been directed into an underground tunnel, but Lake Ülemiste is still the main source of drinking water for the city. According to an old legend, there is a water spirit living in the lake, the Old Man of Ülemiste. From time to time he emerges from the lake, disturbed by the rise of the city close to his abode, and comes down into the city to inquire when Tallinn could be completed. If this should happen one day, the old man would let the lake waters loose and the city with everyone in it would be flooded. Already since very old times, town guards are known to have been instructed to always answer to the water spirit's question that the city is not yet completed, upon which the old man disappointedly returns to the lake. As the development of the city does not seem to stop, even the present residents can confidently tell the old man that the city is far from complete yet. Besides, the lake would no longer be able to bury the whole city, because it has grown far out of proportion compared with its medieval size.

Another legend has it that Lake Ülemiste, which lies directly opposite Tallinn Airport, was born of the tears of Linda, mother of the hero of the national epic *Kalevipoeg*. While carrying stones to the grave of her deceased husband, the mound of Toompea, one of them dropped from her apron. Exhausted and broken, Linda sat down on the boulder and burst into tears over her husband. You can still see Linda's Rock close to the water's edge in Lake Ülemiste.

▽ **Taani kuninga aed (Garden of the Danish King)**

The construction of Tallinn was launched by the Germans and Danes in the 13th century. Some of the first structures erected on **Toompea** were the present St Mary's cathedral and a stone fortress. The so-called small fortress surrounding the keep in the southeastern corner of Toompea was to become the residence of the Danish king, with the rest of the citadel, the big fortress, reserved for the houses of the bishop and the king's vassals. Today the Toompea Palace at the site of the small fortress has been rebuilt several times and serves as the seat of the Republic of Estonia parliament – **Riigikogu**. There are also a number of other institutions of the state, including the seat of the government in Stenbock House, as well as some foreign embassies situated in Toompea. Every day at sunrise, the blue, black and white Estonian national tricolour is hoisted to the tip of the Pikk Hermann (Tall Hermann) Tower, the main tower of the Toompea Castle, and is lowered again at sundown.

An unparalleled attraction in **St Mary's Cathedral** is a rare collection of noblemen's epitaphs in the form of their coats of arms. The cathedral also has the grave monuments of the Swedish army commander Pontus de la Gardie and of the Estonian-born circumnavigator of the globe Adam Johann von Krusenstern.

Opposite the Toompea Castle stands the Russian Orthodox **Alexander Nevsky Cathedral** with its five onion-shaped cupolas. The church was erected as a symbol of Russian power at the end of 19th century when Estonia still belonged to Russia.

Walking in Toompea's short and peaceful streets it is easy to get an

◁ **Toompea Palace, the Parliament House**
◁ **Alexander Nevsky Cathedral**

24

Pikk Jalg △

overview of the area, but a well-informed guide can talk at length about practically every house, most of them former city residences of the Baltic-German landed gentry.

From observation platforms at Toompea's edge there are splendid views of the city. The Kohtu Street platform overlooks the historical centre with its tile roofs and beyond the city with ever new and new high-rises reaching upwards, most of them not ten years old. From the Patkul observation platform the view opens in the direction of the main railway station, the sea and the industrial Kopli area. The outlines of two wooded islands, Naissaar and Aegna, favourite outing places in the summer, are clearly visible on the horizon. The history of both the islands, of which only Naissaar has a few permanent inhabitants, is closely connected with defence of the port of Tallinn. They belonged to a large belt of fortifications erected before World War One but paradoxically turned out to be useless militarywise.

Toompea is the historical heart of Tallinn and the city has grown around

△ **Toomkirik – St Mary's Cathedral**
◁ **St Mary's Cathedral. The pulpit with canopy (Christian Ackermann, 1686)**

△ **Stenbock House,**
  seat of the Estonian government

it over the centuries. The Lower Town, which immediately adjoins Toompea, was earlier on fully surrounded by a town wall built with moats, bastions and fortifications over several centuries. By the 16th century the length of the town wall was 2.4 kilometres and it had more than 40 watchtowers.

The limestone **town wall** was and is mostly 2–3 meters thick and up to 15 meters high. It is

▽ **Town wall**

△ **View of the Lower Town from Toompea**

certainly a peculiarity of Tallinn that the medieval town wall survives to a large extent (1.8 kilometres) with numerous towers. Of its six gate structures, only the towers of the fortified approaches to the Viru and Coast (Ranna) gates and the gate towers in the Pikk jalg (Long Leg) and Lühike jalg (Short Leg) streets survive. These two streets were long the only access routes to Toompea.

▽ **Kohtu Street viewing platform**

△ Paks Margareeta (Fat Margaret) cannon-tower

A good overview of Tallinn's fortifications can be had in the most powerful defence tower of the city – **Kiek in de Kök** (Low German: Look into the Kitchen). The walls of this six-story tower are up to 4.6 metres thick and have 24 artillery positions. The worst tests of Tallinn's fortifications were during the Livionian War when Russian troops laid siege to the city several times. Six stone cannon balls were later walled into the side of Kiek in de Kök facing Harju Hill.

Defence structures of later origin than the town wall, bastions, redoubts and redans, were erected outside the walls from the 16th century onwards. Only the Scania (Rannamäe), Swedish (Lindamäe) and Ingermanland (Harjumäe) bastions were more or less completed.

North end of the Old Town with Oleviste kirik (St Olaf's) overlooking the City Harbour △

The whole complex was surrounded by a zigzagging moat, to which water arrived by a canal from Lake Ülemiste. Later the fate of the fortifications was similar to that of most other fortified cities – their importance began to rapidly decline since the mid-19th century and they started obstructing development of the city. Like any other city, Tallinn needed room as well. Most of the moat was filled up, Snelli tiik (Lake Schnell) being today the only surviving stretch, and a belt of parks was laid out instead of them. Those fortifications that remained in the way of new structures were blasted with the stones reused as construction material. Seeing the fortifications, old town houses and old milieu as something valuable is only a relatively recent phenomenon. The old city of Tallinn in its integrity was listed in 1966, and was entered into the **UNESCO World Heritage List** in 1996.

The cloister at the Dominican Friary ◁
Pühavaimu kirik (Holy Spirit Church) ▷
◁ Kiek in de Kök   Katariina Käik ▽

The 80-hectare **Vanalinn** (Old City) with numerous historical buildings was earlier wholly surrounded with the town wall. Its focal point is **Raekoda** (the Town Hall) with the adjacent Town Hall Square. At Christmastime it is decorated with a tall Christmas tree, while in the summer the square is lined with outdoor cafés and beer gardens. People like to gather in Town Hall Square already with the first sunny days in April.

The first mention of the Tallinn Town Hall in historical records is from 1322. Built in several stages, it is a unique Gothic structure with a slender octagonal console tower and one of the symbols of the city, the Vana Toomas (Old Thomas) weathervane, standing at the tip of its spire. Still attached to a pillar in the Town Hall façade are the stakes – a neck ring and hand rings for the punishment of sinners. Today the Town Hall is the venue of particularly festive receptions and concerts. In the summer concerts are held also in Raekoja plats (Town Hall Square), which is likewise the scene of traditional craft markets and medieval festivals, and cheering crowds have welcomed Estonian Olympic medal winners there.

The atmosphere in the narrow streets and squares of the Old City is truly historical. There are buildings of which separate books have been written and which one could spend a whole day discovering, for example what is left of **Dominiiklaste klooster** (the Dominican Friary) in the quarter between Vene and Müürivahe Streets or **Mustpeade maja** (the House of the Black Heads) at No 26 Pikk Street. There are institutions that have operated for centuries in one and the same location, such as **Raeapteek** (the Town Council Chemist's) that was established in 1422 and is thus one of the oldest in northern Europe.

Raekoda (Town Hall). ▷
It has stood there for 600 years

◁ **Raeapteek** (Town Council Chemist's), selling medicines since 1422
▽ **Raekoja Plats** (Town Hall Square)

The Old City also has numerous rich merchants' houses, guild halls (in Pikk Street), a former Cistercian nunnery and several churches, the most noteworthy of them being Oleviste (St Olaf's), Niguliste (St Nicholas') and Pühavaimu (Holy Spirit) Churches, all of them dating back to the 13th century.

Pühavaimu kirik deserves a visit primarily because of its 15th century double wing altar by the Lübeck painter and woodcarver Bernt Notke. Several of its pastors have left a trace in the Estonian cultural history. So Johann Koell together with the Niguliste pastor Simon Wanradt translated into Estonian the first Lutheran catechism. The book, printed in 1535 in Wittenberg, is the first book in Estonian of which fragments have come down to our days.

In the latter half of the 16th century Balthasar Russow, who served as pastor at Pühavaimu Church, published an important local history source book, the Livonian Chronicle.

Walled into the façade of the church is an attractive baroque clock in a carved wood frame – it has been showing the time to the citizens since the late 17th century.

The slender, 124 m steeple of **Oleviste kirik** (St Olaf's) is perhaps the most conspicuous landmark in Tallinn's skyline. The church has been named after the canonised King Olaf II Haraldsson of Norway. In the Middle Ages Oleviste's tower was higher still – 159 meters, which gave it the title of the world's tallest church at the time, about 1500. Set afire by a bolt of lightning, a common scourge of churches, it was consumed in flames and restored with a somewhat lower spire 130 years later. The observation platform at the base of the spire is the best place for a good overview of the city.

Niguliste kirik (St Nicholas'), dedicated to the patron saint of seafarers and merchants, was first built by German merchants who settled in the Lower Town in the 1230s. The church received a hit in an air raid on March 9, 1944 and burnt down. Most of Harju Street, a 16th century weigh house in Raekoja plats, numerous other historical buildings in various parts of the Old City, as well as large residential areas outside it were also destroyed in the conflagration. The main art treasure of Niguliste, now restored and turned into a museum, is a fabulous 15th century painting, *Dance of Death*, by Bernt Notke. The 7.5-meter-long work is the opening part of a strip of up to fifty figures symbolising the inevitable transience of life.

Vabaduse väljak (Freedom Square) is the traditional parade square of the capital. It is framed with buildings housing the city government, a shady tree-lined avenue leading to Kaarli (Charles') church, the art deco Kunstihoone (Art Building) and Jaani (St John's) church.

△ **Niguliste kirik (St Nicholas' Church)**

◁ **Viru Gate**

View down Lai tänav towards Oleviste kirik (St Olaf's) ▷

△ View of the Russalka Monument from Kadriorg Park

To the east of the city, **Kadriorg** lies on the shore of Tallinn Bay. It boasts an ensemble consisting of a baroque palace and park commissioned by the Russian Tsar Peter I, who dedicated the place to his wife Yekaterina, after whom the whole area has got its name (Ger: Katharinenthal). Peter designed his grand plans in a small cottage standing just under the limestone bluff. It is now installed as a **Peter I Museum**.

The baroque park laid out after drawings by the Italian architect Niccolò Michetti originally had numerous tree-lined walks, flower gardens, fountains, a cascade, lakes and canals. A stylish palace was erected in the park. Several later tsars and members of their families have visited the palace; between the visits it was in use as the governor's summer residence. Then as well as today the park is one of the favourite places where residents and visitors alike love to go for walks in the weekend.

▽ **Kadriorg Palace**

In the 1920s and 30s the Kadriorg Palace was taken into use as the official residence of the Estonian head of state; today the **residence of the Republic of Estonia president** is in a 1930s building forming a harmonious complex with the baroque palace. The Kadriorg Palace, with magnificent stucco decorations in its main hall, houses the **Foreign Art Museum**.

Several buildings connected with the golden period of the park have also been restored. So the former kitchen house now has Johannes Mikkel's private art collection on display. Also in Kadriorg, the 2006-opened KUMU, the fascinating new building of the Estonian Art Museum, exhibits the collection of Estonian art. An area of wooden houses characteristic of Tallinn lies adjacent to Kadriorg Park. **Lauluväljak**, the Song Festival Ground, lies to the east of Kadriorg, in the direction of Pirita. The tradition of all-Estonian song festivals was established in the country in 1869. The present choir stand, which accommodates up to 30,000 singers, was built for the song festival of 1960. Lauluväljak has an important role in the restoration of Estonian independence. Ushering in the Singing Revolution in 1988, people gathered there to sing patriotic songs and to fly the blue, black and white national flags that had been prohibited for decades by the occupation authorities. A few kilometres to the west of the city **Eesti Vabaõhumuuseum** (the Estonian Open-Air Museum) at Rocca al Mare gives a good overview of the Estonian traditional rural architecture and life in the 19th–20th centuries.

KUMU, the Estonian Art Museum, interior view ▷
KUMU, with the president's residence and ▽
Kadriorg Palace in the background

Song Festival Grounds

North and Northeast Estonia

Pakri Peninsula

The windy Pakri Peninsula, 50 km to the west of Tallinn, rises from the sea with the historical Pakri lighthouse at its farthest tip. The bluff, locally called *pank*, arches around the whole peninsula, being the steepest between the town of Paldiski and Cape Pakri. This is the longest stretch along Estonia's northern coast where the weaves break right against the rocks. The view opening from the bluff is unique for Estonia. Its imposing profile, with a sheer fall of up to 25 meters to the waves below, makes this one the most striking places to admire the bluff.

Two islands, **Suur-Pakri** and **Väike-Pakri**, respectively the Big and the Small Pakri Islands, are clearly in view from the western edge of the peninsula. For centuries they were a settlement area of Estonian Swedes, of whom there were about 350 on the islands by the late 1930s. Before and in the course of World War II the population was forced to leave the islands, most of them settling in Sweden. After the war the Soviets used the islands' alvars as a target for bombing practice and there were several military units permanently located on the islands. Former village sites overgrown with bushes, dry-stone walls and the partly tidied ruins of a church on Suur-Pakri create an atmosphere permeated with memories of old times.

The town of Paldiski stands on the western coast of the peninsula where the deep ice-free bay serves as a splendid natural harbour. Looking for the site of a naval base in his newly conquered lands, Tsar Peter I of Russia launched the construction of a port at Paldiski in earnest. He personally laid the corner stone to the town in 1723. The town, the port and the castle, which partly survives until today, were built with the labour of convicts, including many participants in a Russian late 18th century peasant revolt. Although construction work went on for half a century in Paldiski and on the Väike-Pakri Island directly across the bay, the plan of locking entrance to the bay by means of a gigantic pier was never accomplished. Thousands of convicts worked themselves to exhaustion at the construction

◁ **The bluff at Parki**

The bluff, rising to 25 m from the sea, runs all round Cape Pakri ▽

site and died, and loads upon loads of limestone were buried into the waters, all in vain.

During the Soviet occupation Paldiski became a no trespassing military territory with a submarine training and repair base, including two nuclear reactors. As a reminder of that period the training centre building measuring a couple of hundred meters down the front still guards the entrance to the city. Today, Paldiski with its two harbours is an important export port for timber, scrap metal, peat etc. The main shipping routes link Paldiski with Finland, Sweden and Germany.

Keila-Joa

Keila-Joa (Keila Falls) is one of the most scenic places in Estonia. The main magnet, which has given the name to the place, is a waterfall where the Keila River drops six metres from a ledge of 60-70 metres across. Layers of greenish sandstone and brownish slate are exposed at the ledge under a strong upper layer of limestone. From the falls to the sea the river has carved a canyon of about 15 meters deep. A free-style park of approximately 80 hectares with beautiful views of Keila-Joa Hall lies to both sides of the river.

△ Vasalemma Hall

▽ Keila-Joa (Keila Falls)

△ Osmussaar Island

The Gothic Revival manor hall stands on the right bank of the river with glorious views of the falls and the **park** opening from its windows. It was built in the 1830s by Alexander von Benckendorff, founder of the imperial secret police in imperial Russia. Even Tsar Nicholas I honoured the housewarming party with his presence. In the 19th century the manor hall passed through marriage to the well-known Volkonsky family. Representatives of both the lines are buried in the family graveyard near the park.

In the Soviet occupation period the manor hall was at the disposal of the military, who fenced in the whole area, barring access to it by the public. Most of the ancillary buildings that once belonged to the ensemble have been mutilated by rebuilding, and the hall itself is in need of a caring master.

Approaching Tallinn along the coastline from Keila-Joa the ground rises rapidly. The clint comes closer and closer to the sea and reaches its highest point of 31 meters above sea level at **Türisalu Pank**. A beautiful view of the sea opens from the cliff edge, particularly at sunset.

Padise

In its earlier history Padise has been an important settlement in western Harju County and has a number of historical and architectural monuments — a hill fort, ruins of a Cistercian abbey, and a partly renovated manor complex. The Padise hill fort from the 1st millennium AD lies on a mound of about 14 meters in a bend of the Kloostri River, about one kilometre south of the castle ruins.

The house was established at the beginning of the 14th century when Cistercian monks moved to Padise form Dünamünde (now Daugavgrīva in Latvia). With intervals, it took more than 200 years to build the complex. The original wooden monastic buildings were burnt down in the course of the Estonians' last major effort to put up a resistance to the foreign domination, St George's Night Revolt of 1343.

In its place a fortified abbey was built wholly of stone, with the local limestone, called Vasalemma marble, used as its building material. The rectangular complex had a chapel, a church, a gate tower, several other defence towers and numerous other rooms the monks needed to lead their lives. The configuration of the moat surrounding the abbey, with drawbridges leading across it, can clearly be observed even today. The location of fishponds dug by the monks can be discerned north of the highway. The abbey was last used as a fortification in the Livonian War. For a few years it was even held

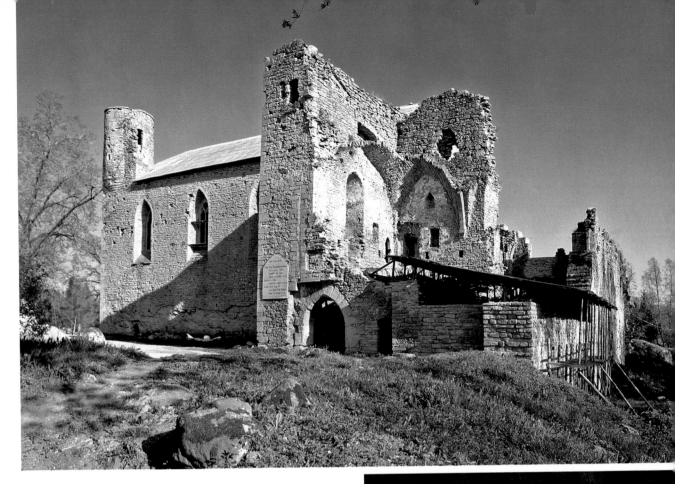

by the Russians. In the Swedish period and after the Great Northern War the local manor lords used the buildings as residential and household premises. In 1622 King Gustavus II Adolphus gave the monastery to Mayor of Riga Thomas von Ramm. The complex stands in ruins since a fire in 1766. Long-time Padise manor lords, descendants of Thomas von Ramm, built a new baroque mansion next to the ruins and gradually erected new and new ancillary buildings to both sides of the Kloostri River.

There is a legend about a stick Peter I had given to the von Ramms. The tsar, so the story goes, had used it to beat the baron when the latter refused to sell grain to the state. During a break in the beating the baron had managed to say that he did not intend to *sell* the grain, but give it to the state. Peter had then made up with the baron and given him his stick as a present.

By today the von Ramms have bought back their family estate expropriated from them in 1919.

Padise, ruins of Cistercian abbey △
▷

△ St Mary's of Jõelähtme, 14th c with early 20th c tower

Saha Chapel △

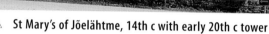

Rebala Conservation Area

The area east of Tallinn was the most densely populated part of prehistoric Harju County, and some of its most expressive features today make up the Rebala Conservation Area. Some historians believe that the ancient **Rebala Village** has given us the name of Rävala, by which the land around present-day Tallinn was known before the foreign conquest, and through it also to the city of Reval, today's Tallinn. Permanent settlement in the area goes back to about 3,000 years ago and also the prehistoric fields discovered there are of the same age, being the oldest such cultivated patches in the East-European forest belt. The forests, which earlier grew in the area, were cut down and burnt. The thin soil on the limestone bedrock was well suited for cultivation and so the density of settlement continued to increase in the Rebala area. There are more than 200 stone cyst graves, 80 cult stones and several settlement sites scattered in the fields and pastures in Rebala. Finds from old graves provide proof that ancient Estonians had close commer-

◁ Rebala stone cist graves from
the 1st millenium BC

◁ Karst area where the Jõelähtme River flows underground for most of the year

cial contacts with the other Nordic countries. A museum at Jõelähtme right beside the motor road leading to St Petersburg provides an overview of the history of the area. Outside there are some reconstructed prehistoric Estonians' stone cist graves on display.

Besides, the Rebala Conservation Area has a number of other archaeological and architectural monuments, the most conspicuous of them being the Jõesuu hill fort, the sacrificial site of **Ülgase pank**, the 15th century **Saha Chapel**, the 17th to 18th century **Maardu Hall**, **Jõelähtme Church** and a stage.

In the middle reaches of the Jõelähtme River (River Source River) between Kostivere and the highway there is a conveniently situated karst area, where the river flows for nearly 2.5 kilometres under the ground, with the riverbed featuring numerous crevices and funnels. The riverbed is dry for most of the year, but in the spring it is flooded and loud. Waters pressing up from under the ground cause sounds as if of someone slurping or sighing. The source of the river, actually the place where it resurfaces, has given the name to the whole parish.

Jägala Falls

Of natural falls, Jägala, with a drop of 8.1 meters, is the highest in Estonia. The river is nearly 100 kilometres long and together with its tributaries drains a predominantly wooded and wetland area, ensuring a sufficient flow even in the summer low water period. Dropping from the ledge, the water has eroded away soft sandstones under the upper limestone layers and so the ledge projects forward, providing an opportunity to the audacious to scramble across the river behind the falling curtain of water. It is a feat that cannot be recommended, however, as the falls retreat at the average speed of 2–3 centimetres a year as the result of bits of stone falling from the top. A canyon of several hundred metres with rapids on its floor over quite a distance remains as a witness of the falls' retreat. The power of the falling water has earlier been used in several watermills, and later electric power stations situated both up and down river from the falls. The Linnamäe hydroelectric power plant near the estuary of the river has now been restored. When it was completed in the 1930s it was regarded as one of the most beautiful industrial structures in Estonia. Close to the falls stand tenements of a former pulp mill. Downstream from the falls, also standing on the right bank of the river, is the Jõesuu hill fort, one of the biggest in Estonia with a territory of 3.5 hectares, rising above the reservoir of the new power plant.

▽ **Jägala Falls**

Witches' Well at Tuhala, where high water makes an underground river "boil over"

Lahemaa National Park

At the boundary line of Viru and Harju Counties the more of less straight coastline suddenly becomes deeply indented. Peninsulas alternate with bays, with stony headlands and shoals stretching far out to the sea. Toward the inland, the most important fault line in the landscape is the limestone escarpment, the Baltic Clint, here mostly buried under later sediments and revealed in the relief in the form of gradual descending terraces. Coastal formations from different periods of the Baltic Sea can be met at every pace, as well as huge boulders, some of them sitting right at the water's edge while others are hidden deep in the forest. This is Lahemaa, Land of Bays, as the Finnish geographer Johannes Gabried Granö aptly first called it in 1922. Thanks to the institution of a national park in the area in 1971 Lahemaa's nature has been thoroughly studied and there is public access to large parts of it, with signposts guiding to interesting sites and nature trails laid out to others.

△ **Viitna Inn**　　　　　**Lake Viitna Suurjärv** ▷

Viitna

Thanks to its location at a crossing of roads, Viitna, the gateway to Lahemaa, was known already in medieval times. It was the natural place for an **inn**, a symbol of Viitna even today. The old post road between Tallinn and Viitna once had a total of 25 inns, one per every three kilometres. In earlier times fairs were held at Viitna three times a year, with peasants from all over North Estonia meeting there. Characteristic of the Viitna fair, it is told, was the sound of the honing of scythes, as everyone buying a scythe tested its quality by the sound of the hone against it.

The restored Viitna Inn is a long building with a rectangular ground plan and a high hip roof. Originally there were two stables under the same roof but today the only memory of them is a hitching beam at the entrance.

South of the crossing by the side of the road leading to Kadrina lie the **Viitna Lakes**. The name of Linajärv (Lake Flax), also known as Viitna Väikejärv (Small Lake of Viitna) derives from the fact that local farmers earlier used it for retting the flax.

According to folk tradition Viitna Suurjärv (Big Lake of Viitna) is a place where the horse of Kalevipoeg, the hero of the Estonian national epic, had once wallowed, and even the shape of the lake is said to refer to it.

Palmse

The renovated baroque manor complex of Palmse comprising more than 20 houses and a park of 18 hectares has become one of the symbols of the Lahemaa National Park. It houses the Park administration and information point. A hotel and restaurant are open in the old distillery. The earlier history of the manor is connected with Cistercian monks. Sine 1676 until its expropriation by the Republic of Estonia (1919) it belonged to von der Pahlens. That old line, which today continues in Germany, has brought a lot of glory to Palmse.

Areal view of the Palmse manor complex ▽

The manor hall rises directly ahead as you enter through the main gate. The stable and coach house stand to the left and the storehouse to the right, with the administrator's house a little farther away. The manor hall, traditionally divided into the landlord's and the landlady's wings, was built in 1782–85 by the architect J C Mohr. Nowadays the mansion functions as a manor hall-museum where also concerts are held. The well pavilion and the spring pavilion stand between the main building and the administrator's house. The onion-shaped dome of the latter looks strange at first, but can be understood when we recall that von der Pahlens were statesmen and soldiers whose career was closely linked with the Tsar's court and St Petersburg, and they apparently attempted to copy elements of Russian architecture at home. The bathing house, one of the most beautiful buildings in the park, stands on the bank of the lake. The structure was probably also used to accommodate summer guests. The bathing area was between the bathing house and the rotunda, a feature quite widespread in Estonian manor parks in the first half of the 19th century. There is a small coffee house at the upper lake where the lord and the lady were usually served coffee after walks in the park.

The Palmse Park with lakes and the river flowing through the park was fashioned into a free-style English forest park in the 19th century. The landscaping took advantage of the varying relief, and long kilometres of park paths – 35 km in Palmse, of which 11 km have been

Folk music festival at Palmse ▷
Palmse Hall. The ballroom ▽

△ **Palmse. Bathing house and rotunda**

restored by the National Park – were laid out; also bridges across riverbeds and romantic pavilions were built.

One of the many park paths leads to a large group of erratic boulders called **Kloostrikivid** (Monastery Stones). The group, carried to the place by continental ice from near Vyborg, consists of thirteen boulders more than 10 meters across and a large number of smaller ones. There is a legend that these rosy-coloured so-called bog stone boulders are actually petrified devils who had turned into stones from a long wait for the nuns of the former St Michaels' Nunnery of Tallinn to return to their earlier holding. Let legends remain legends but for the Baltic-German academician Gregor Helmersen (1803–1885) this group of boulders was one of several that helped him work out the theory of continental icing. Together with the then owner of Palmse manor, chairman of the Estonian Nobility Corporation Alexander von der Pahlen, a man interested in geology, he studied a number of large erratic boulders in Lahemaa and raised the issue of the need for their protection. As for the manor lord, he was interested in fossils, and even made his nine children look for them. His most sensational find, the world's oldest fossilised sea urchin, is now kept at the Estonian Natural History Museum in Tallinn.

The one-time owners of Palmse are buried at the Ilumäe Chapel ▽

▽ **Kloostrikivid (Monastery Stones)**

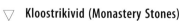

Muuksi

The **Muuksi hill fort** is one of the most panoramic observation points in the Lahemaa National Park, rising to 47 meters above sea level. A thousand years ago there was an ancient Estonians' hill fort at the place; later the hill has been used to frolic around the bonfire on St John's Eve, the traditional midsummer festival. In independent Estonia before World War Two the bonfire came to mark Victory Day (June 23), the anniversary of victory over the Baltic-German Landeswehr army in the War of Independence, and the custom of the Victory Day flame brought by horsemen developed. From the high promontory the fire could be seen in villages a long distance away.

A stone memorial symbolising three military history circumstances connected with Finland stands on the hill fort. Above all it is a curtsey to the Finnish volunteers who fought in the Estonian War of Independence. Secondly it is a bow to the Erna scout group of Estonians trained in Finland who crossed the Gulf of Finland in the early stages of World War II in 1941 and laid the basis to an armed resistance movement in the Red Army rear. Thirdly, it pays homage to the so-called Finland volunteers, the roughly 3,500 Estonians who fought in

Muuksi hill fort △
Stone cist graves ▷
Seashore strewn with erratic boulders ▽

△ **Kolga Hall**

the Finnish army in World War II and returned to Estonia in 1944 with the hope of restoring Estonia's independence.

Heading towards Loo from Muuksi we come to the biggest **stone cist graves** in Estonia. Known as Hundikangrud (Wolf Barrows), the barrows have mostly been heaped up of limestone rubble picked from the fields where the plough had brought them to the surface during cultivation. The name stone cist grave has been given to this type of burials after a cist of limestone slabs in the centre of the grave. About 500 stone cist barrows have been found in the country, most of them situated in northern Estonia and Saaremaa. The barrows lie on higher ground from where there is an extensive view of the surroundings, often of the sea or a lake. Outwardly, a stone cist grave is a circle of closely laid stones under the turf, usually from 8 to 13 meters in diameter, with the height varying from 30 centimetres to one and a half metres. The most important part of the interior structure is the stone cist oriented in the north-southerly direction. In older graves the cist was built of limestone slabs set on the edge, but in later ones it is of limestone slabs or granite boulders laid like a dry-stone wall. The cist was covered with slabs of limestone and smaller stones heaped on the top.

Kolga Manor

After the Danes conquered North Estonia, the lands of Kolga were enfeoffed to the Roma Cistercian Nunnery situated on Gotland Island. Proof of this is found in a record dating from 1259 in which King Erik V (Klipping) of Denmark confirmed the holding to the Roma monks. Kolga belonged to the Cistercians until 1510 when it was exchanged for King Christian's holdings in Denmark. Among the next owners one of the most prominent men was Pontus de la Gardie, Vice-Regent of Tallinn and Livonia, a man whose granddaughter married State Admiral Count Gustav Otto von Stenbock. The Stenbocks ruled Kolga for more than 300 years. Since the last land reform of the early 1990s the manor hall is again in the possession of the same family.

A century ago a huge area of about 50,000 hectares was ruled from Kolga. Nearly 8,000 peasants lived within its boundaries. Kolga manor owned several auxiliary manors and inns, a port, a brewery, distillery and numerous traditional farm buildings.

A restaurant is open on the ground floor of the manor hall that was given its Classical appearance in the 1820s and is now being renovated. The former stables now house a hotel and the post office and also some other buildings are in use in the summer season.

Viinistu

The stony Cape Purekkari on Pärispea Peninsula is the northernmost point of the Estonian mainland, lying at 59°40'30" North. Pärispea is remarkable for its large number of big **erratic boulders** – Odakivi, Tiirukivi, Mustkivi etc. According to folk tradition the boulders are all connected with stone throwing contests between the hero of the national epic, Kalevipoeg, and the Old Heathen, the embodiment of evil. Most settlements on the peninsula lie along the coasts, the interior being relatively deserted. A good example of how a former Soviet fishery has been given new lease of life in a totally novel function can be witnessed at **Viinistu**. Businessman Jaan Manitski, who was born in the village, has turned the former fish-smoking unit of the fishery into an **art gallery**. Auxiliary buildings now function as a guesthouse and restaurant and some halls that still stand empty are used to give performances in the summer. Permanently exhibited in the art gallery are several hundred paintings ranging from classical to modern Estonian art from Jaan Manitski's private collection. The level of the gallery, quite comparable to state museums, has made the small coastal village into a notable Estonian art centre.

Net sheds at the shore in Altja △

△ Altja Inn

Käsmu ▽

△ Sagadi manor complex

Sagadi Hall

The road from Palmse to Sagadi passes through a forest called Riidsoo nõmm (Strife Bog Heath). The name refers to constant quarrels between the owners of Palmse and Sagadi manors over the border that used to run through that place. The manor hall itself lies in a limestone plane surrounded by fields where flights of cranes gather in the autumn before setting out to the south.

◁ Gatehouse of the manor (1794)

▽ Forestry Museum in former stables

Sagadi Hall (1793–95) △
Enfilade ▷

Sagadi's first written mention is of 1469, although the manor could have existed before. For a longer period (1687–1919) it belonged to von Focks, many of whom were soldiers and leading officials of the provincial administration.

The present manor hall was built in 1749. At the end of the same century the rococo building was extended and given a Classical façade. Neo-Classical ceiling-pieces from the second half of the 19th century have been restored in the interior. The vestibule has the central position in the house and the festive hall with a painted ceiling lies immediately behind it. Sagadi Hall is fitted with restored furniture. It functions as a conference centre and concerts and theatrical performances take place there. The manor complex consists of about ten more buildings, including a grand gatehouse, a park and a lake with islands. The restored cattle house accommodates a forestry museum, a hotel and restaurant, and a children's nature school is open in the former distillery. The early Classical gatehouse of 1794 with limestone tablets in memory of the manor owners' ancestors fastened to its walls has become a visiting card of the manor.

A sign-posted nature trail provides a convenient way of learning to know the interesting and variable neighbourhood, including traces of the activity of local wildlife (bear, elk, wild boar).

Viru Bog

There are thousands of wetlands in Estonia, making up more than one fifth of the whole territory of the country. The Viru Bog of only 150 hectares in size is one of the smallest but, thanks to a boardwalk through it, one of the most visited ones. Wetlands and bogs, the latter being a concrete type of wetland, develop in places where there is too much water and poor drainage. Viru Bog was formed when a former lake grew over about 5,000 years ago.

Peat grows and disintegrates in bogs, seeping up moving surface water. The peculiarity of bogs is that they only feed on rainwater. It is said that a bog, which actually consists of 85–90 percent of water, is like a body of water on which you cannot sail and like dry land on which you cannot travel either on horseback or in a wagon. The most important difference from a usual water body is that the large mass of water is generally not visible in a bog. The water moves extremely slowly in the peat deposit and the bog holds water like a huge sponge. The height of that sponge in the Viru Bog, for example, is up to six meters. The soil of the bog, poor in nutrients, only supports a few, extremely hardy plants. The most widespread of them are peat mosses, the plants that a bog actually consists of. On your walk through the bog you can study the main bog plants, such as bog pine, birch, bob whortleberry, marsh rosemary, cranberry, cloudberry, the insect-eating sundew, etc.

The Viru Bog nature trail passes several pools. You can go ahead and taste the bog water. Despite its brownish colour it is the purest water available in nature. The brown colour is due to humus matter – products of the disintegration of peat moss – dissolved in the water. The low mineral content of the water influences its taste. *Laukad* (pools) and *älved* (wet patches) are only found in bogs. The first are open, the others hidden pools with very sparse plant cover. The length of the nature trail in the Viru Bog is 3.5 kilometres. If possible it is recommendable to have a bus or car waiting for you at the end of the trail.

Rakvere

The heart and main sight in Rakvere, the central town of the Lääne-Viru (West-Viru) County, is a hill fort (**Vallimägi**) where ancient Estonians had a stronghold at the beginning of the 13th century. In written records it is first mentioned under the name of Tarvanpää in the Livonian Chronicle of Henricus de Lettis in 1226. In the 13th century the Danes built the fortified Wesenberg Castle at the site of the ancient stronghold, surrounding it with a wall of stone and erecting a few stone buildings within its perimeter. From the Danes the castle passed on to the Teutonic Order in 1346 and then to the Livonian Order; in the next century a big and powerful stone fortress was erected on the present Vallimägi. The chequered history of the castle, marked by sieges and conquests, ended in a Polish-Swedish war at the beginning of the 17th century, upon which it was struck off the list of fortifications. An unusual siege is mentioned from 1574. During the Livonian War Russians had taken hold of the castle and it was being besieged by Swedes and Germans. Also Scots took part in the siege as mercenaries. The chronicler brings a rather detailed description how the Germans and the Scots got into a row. A battle of just one hour outside the walls of the Wesenberg Castle remained the last one for as many as 1,500 Scots. Some of them, 70 in number, managed to yield themselves prisoner to the Russians in the castle – only to meet their end slightly later in Moscow.

Today there is a castle museum on Vallimägi. Existence of the castle served as a precondition for the establishment of a settlement at the foot of the castle and in the vicinity. Rakvere was granted a city charter in 1302, about half a century after the stone fortress was built. The settlement was first limited to just one street (today's Pikk Street) at the eastern side of the castle, leading from north to south. Today the Rakvere Castle is surrounded with buildings from all sides. The streets in its closest neighbourhood still follow the original pattern. The bronze figure of an aurochs standing on Vallimägi is a symbol of the town.

Rakvere is the only town in Estonia where a saint has been buried. The Orthodox priest Sergius Florinski, killed by the Bolsheviks in 1918, was canonised in 2002 and his remains were reburied in the church of the Birth of the Virgin Mary in Rakvere.

Friedrich Reinhold Kreutzwald, a central figure in Estonian cultural history, author of the national epic *Kalevipoeg*, lived at **Sõmeru** near

Tarvas, the aurochs, a symbol of Rakvere ▽

59

Rakvere in 1804–17. An erratic boulder marks the playground of his childhood – the future writer is said to have liked to sit on it when herding cattle. The boulder, called Kroonikivi (the Crown Stone), now has a concrete crown one metre in diameter – there is an Estonian saying that the herd boy was the king to his hoofed subjects.

◁ **Ruins of the Rakvere Order Castle**
◁ **Rakvere.**
   Fountain in Turuplats (Market Square)

Paide

Paide lies in the heart of Estonia – so claim the signposts the traveller sees as he approaches the city. In fact, Paide is situated close to the geographical centre of Estonia. The town was established in 1265 when a castle of the Livonian order was built at a crossroads there. The historical core of the town is made up of **Vallimägi** (Castle Hill) with ruins of the castle and the main tower as well as the historical quarter to the southeast of the Castle Hill.

Central Square with the Holy Cross Church ▽

Vallimägi is today the venue of various outdoor activities, a place where both local people and tourists like to go for a stroll. Vallitorn (the Castle Keep) suffered badly in the last war and has now been restored, being used as a museum, exhibition space and café. There are several limestone sculptures on Vallimägi, a monument to St John's Night Revolt (1343) and a choir stand. Paide's central square, lined with one-storey houses on three sides, is quite well proportioned. **Püha Risti kirik** (Church of the Holy Cross) with late Classical elements on the northern side of the square stands out among Estonian churches because its tower is not situated at the west end of the building as usual but in the middle. The most outstanding structures in Paide are the church with big old weeping birches on either side of the steeple and the late Art Nouveau Town Hall in the central square, which received its present appearance after reconstruction in 1920.

Paide is also known by its Limestone Days, an event dedicated to the Estonian national stone and triggered perhaps by a dolomite quarry at Mündi close to the town. Prominent sculptors have taken part in the limestone carving days and as a result numerous limestone sculptures now decorate the town. A hundred metres from the central square stands *Paesümfoonia* (Limestone Symphony)

Paide. Restored Castle Keep (Vallitorn) on Castle Hill (Vallimägi) △

by Riho Kuld, marking the birthplace of Arvo Pärt, an Estonian composer famed throughout the world.

The Reopalu cemetery at the western edge of the town is the last resting place of the prominent linguist and local history researcher August Wilhelm Hupel (1737–1819). He studied life in the Baltic countries, their history and geography, compiled the first Estonian grammar and the biggest German-Estonian dictionary of the period. Hupel worked long as pastor at Põltsamaa, but spent the last fifteen years of his life in Paide.

Birthplace of the Writer Anton Hansen Tammsaare

The writer the Estonians respect perhaps the most and whose works authentically express the Estonian character is Anton Hansen Tammsaare (1878–1940). The **writer's birthplace** on Põhja-Tammsaare Farm in Vetepere Village in the Albu Commune is the location of his most important novel, *Truth and Justice*. The novel, where the farm has

Vargamäe. Birthplace of the writer A H Tammsaare ▽

been given the name of Vargamäe, describes the life and aspirations of several generations in a lonely village in the depth of forests, incessant fighting with excess water, stones, the neighbour's pranks and above all themselves. The Tammsaare "field hill" is a longish drumlin rising like a loaf of bread above the surrounding swampy forests. This was Tammsaare's childhood home (Hill Farm in the novel) that was restored and opened as the author's house museum in 1958. The museum gives a graphic picture of life on the farm at the beginning of the 20th century. In the summer open-air performances are staged at the writer's birthplace.

Jäneda

The oldest record of the village is of 1353, and of the Jäneda estate of 1510. The present two-storied red brick Art Nouveau **Jäneda Hall** was built in 1915. The numerous outhouses of the manor – the distillery, grain drier, stables, smithy, cattle houses and storehouse mainly go back to the 18th and the 19th centuries, with most of them lining the drive leading from the manor to the highway. They are all in a one style, based on decorative use of split granite boulders, dolomite and red brick.

The wooden hunting lodge, which is also the former school, is situated on the bank of Lake Kalijärv, half a kilometre to the southwest of the manor seat. The well-known English writer Herbert George Wells stayed there in August 1934, visiting an acquaintance of his, Maria Zakarevskaya-Benckendorff-Budberg. The baroness had close relations also with the Russian author Maxim Gorky and the British diplomat Robert Bruce Lockhart. A display at the **Jäneda Museum** in the main building of the manor sheds light on the colourful life of the local landlords and gives an overview of the agricultural school that has operated there for many years.

Today Jäneda Hall and its annex house a **consultancy centre for farmers**. The manor hall also has an ingenious **musical observatory** containing musical instruments, a telescope and planetarium, installed on the initiative of the composer Urmas Sisask, whose music is inspired by the starry sky.

The well-kept Jäneda manor park with large open areas, lakes and old trees has today been extensively reconstructed.

Heath ▷
Lake Paukjärv ▽

▽ **Jäneda Hall**

Oil Shale Area

Hills of ash and waste rising high from the ground alternating with chimneys and giant industrial facilities form the typical scenery in East Virumaa. We have come to the oil shale country, the only mining area in Estonia. Estonia is unique in the world for the fact that 90 percent of the electricity is generated by burning oil shale, a fuel of relatively low calorie content. Oil shale and electricity generation provide livelihood to every fifth person in the East-Viru County.

Oil shale mining in eastern Virumaa started in 1916. The village of Kukruse lying between Kohtla-Järve and Jõhvi has given the Estonian oil shale its scientific name — kukersite. The stone now being used as fuel was created from deposits of algae that settled on the floor of an Ordovician Sea. The organic matter content in oil shale is 15 to 70 percent and the layers of oil shale, which can be up to 70 cm think, lie alternately with those of limestone in the ground.

Oil shale is extracted both from underground mines and quarries. In mining the mass of rock is transported to the ground and then concentrated, limestone being separated from kukersite. This process inevitably produces large amounts of solid waste, which is deposited in numerous waste hills. The ash and waste hills of Kiviõli and Kohtla-Järve are considered to be the highest man-made features of relief in the Baltic countries, reaching as high as 115–120 meters from the ground.

The **Oil Shale Museum** in Kohtla-Järve and the **Mining Museum** in Kohtla give a good overview of oil shale mining and the accompanying problems. At the Kohtla Museum the visitors are invited to try all the usual miner's work, beginning with donning their overalls, riding to work by underground train, testing the various boring and transport techniques and ending with an invigorating lunch of soup in an underground canteen.

Kunda △
Limestone quarry △
Mining Museum ▽

◁ **Ash hill in the oil shale country**
◁ **Purtse Castle**
◁ **Ruins of Toolse Castle**

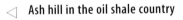

Virumaa Clint

One of Estonia's most magnificent natural monuments is no doubt the North-Estonian limestone escarpment, the Baltic Clint. Many artists and poets have rendered the abrupt end of the level and open landscape before reaching the Gulf of Finland. The expanse of the sea can nowhere be viewed from as high as from the windy Ontika Pank. On a clear day it is possible to see the islands of Suur and Väike Tütarsaar (Great and Lesser Tyuters) and Suursaar (Hogland). Before World War II these islands belonged to Finland, but are now under Russian administration. The limestone cliffs have been regarded as the foremost symbol of Estonian nature. The cliffs with stormy waves breaking underneath them are depicted on the Estonian 100-kroon banknote.

The extensive **Baltic Clint**, which starts at Lake Ladoga in northwestern Russia and ends at the southern shore of Sweden, has a total length of about 1,200 kilometres. In Estonia it can be observed over a distance of three hundred kilometres from Virumaa to Cape Pakri. It is the highest in the stretch between Saka and Toila, rising to 56 meters above sea level at Ontika. This is the most outstanding stretch of the Estonian section of the clint, where it comes to within a hundred meters from the sea. The base of the clint is of Cambrian blue clays and sandstones, the middle part being made up of Ordovician sandstones and slates and the upper part of stratified limestone deposits. So the profile of the cliff opens a geological archive spanning nearly 100 million years. The rocks forming the cliff settled about 570–470 million years ago. The vegetation at the foot of the cliff is in sharp contrast with the level and open landscape on the cliff — primeval-looking woods of broadleaved trees, talus and springs, the soil covered with moss, rotten trunks of trees and tall ferns. For several kilometres there is often not a single pathway leading down from the escarpment. Earlier, when there were more coastal fishermen, special winches were used to haul up the catch and fishing gear.

It is possible to descend from the cliff at **Valaste**, the location of the highest **falls** in Estonia. The place is provided with an observation platform, but the 26-metre falls has abundant water only in the spring, contracting to a trickle in the summer. The brownish colour of the water refers to the bogs of the neighbourhood.

In all there are more than 30 falls and cascades dropping down the Estonian clint, but most of them are quite small.

◁ **Valaste Falls, the highest in Estonia**

Toila-Oru

The Toila-Oru settlement lies at mouth of the River Pühajõgi (Holy River). The free-style park, one of the grandest in North Estonia, is almost English in character, with about 300 species of plants growing in a territory of nearly 70 hectares, most of them various exotic species of European origin, but including also species from the Far East and America. Many of the species were introduced in the first half of the 20th century from Russia and Germany. Several small architectural pieces, such as a grotto, the Silver Spring Cave and terraces with support walls can still be seen in the park. The Nõiametsa (Witches' Wood) Pavilion with a fine view in the direction of Narva Bay has been restored. The palace around which the splendid park was laid out unfortunately no longer exists. The palace, known from many old picture postcard albums as a white three-storey edifice, was completed in 1899, commissioned by the rich Russian merchant Grigory Yeliseyev. Left ownerless as a result of the Russian Revolution, it was taken into use in 1935 as the Estonian president's summer residence, but was destroyed in the course of World War II. Only bits of masonry survive of the former mansion but even these give a vague idea of the former grandeur of the palace. Buildings (gatehouse etc) that once belonged to the palace ensemble are gradually being reconstructed.

Oru, once the site of a grand palace

Sinimäed
(Blue Hills)

The location of the Blue Hills in a narrow passage between the Gulf of Finland and the Alutaguse marshes makes it possible to control the Tallinn-Narva road – a circumstance that has given the hills strategic importance. Numerous bloody battles have been fought for control of the hills.

Attackers have come from both directions during the history. To notice the approach of hostile forces in good time Russians erected a guard tower in the Blue Hills during the Great Northern War at the beginning of the 18th century. In World War One the Russians built advance fortifications of St Petersburg there, with ammunition cellars and defence structures erected on the easternmost hill, Pargimägi (Park Hill). In World War II it was the scene of the bloodiest battles in Estonian history.

In spring 1944 the Narva River and Sinimäed were one of the main sections of hostilities on the whole eastern front. The Red Army concentrated into the 50 km section of the front 25 divisions and numerous armoured units. For Germany it was important to hold the front mainly because it wanted to keep the supply channel of oil and petrol on the basis of local oil shale. Estonians, Flemings, Norwegians, and Danes fought side by side with the Germans there. In the turmoil of heavy battles the front stood in the vicinity of Narva for a total of eight months, of this for three months, from July to September 1944, directly at the Blue Hills. The German Tannenberg defence line built from the Blue Hills to the sea remained unconquered. But German

Sinimäed, site of fierce battles in World War II △
German war cemetery in Toila △

troops were forced to retreat in September as the danger emerged that they could otherwise be closed into a sack from the south. If the battles for Narva lasted a total of eight months, then after the Blue Hills were abandoned the rest of Estonia fell to the Russians within just a few weeks.

The total number of victims of the battles fought between Narva and the Blue Hills amounted to about 200,000 and are thus comparable with the Verdun and Somme battles of World War I. Even today live ordnance comes to the surface from the ground, trenches and bunkers can be seen here and there, and the crosses at the old Vaivara Cemetery are chipped with bullets. As soldiers of many nations fell in the battles, different monuments have been erected there – a cemetery of Soviet soldiers for nearly 15,000 fallen with a memorial obelisk, monuments to Norwegians and Flemings, as well as a memorial cross to Estonian soldiers who were forced to fight on both sides in the war – Estonians had been mobilised also by the Soviets in World War II. A perimeter wall of the old cemetery has been restored and memorial tablets to different units are being added to it all the time. Opening of a war museum in the Blue Hills is being planned. A closer look at the Blue Hills can be had from a sign-posted trail of 4–5 kilometres passing through the one-time battleground.

◁ Stone cross (1590) in memory of Vasili Rosladen, a Russian boyar

Narva

The history of no city in Estonia has been as contradictory and changeful as that of Narva. Already the Vikings used the historical border river flowing past the city as a waterway. According to the Novgorod Chronicle there was a ford in the river here since 1172 and a small fortress surrounded with a wall and a moat was erected to defend it. A bigger trading settlement sprang up at the crossing and in 1345 King Waldemar IV of Denmark issued a privilege granting it the Charter of Lübeck. After Northern Estonia was sold to the Livonian Order in the same year the old Danish *castellum* was rebuilt into a powerful keep and the erection of a belt of fortifications around it began. When the Russians built their fortress of Ivangorod on the opposite bank of the river in 1492, the castle was further fortified, the height of the main tower, Pikk Hermann, being increased to 50 meters. After the name of the main tower the whole castle came to be called the Hermann Castle. The victory of the Swedish army under Charles XII over the Russians in a battle for Narva in 1700 is still remembered by a monument with the Swedish lion in Narva. But in 1704 Russia conquered Narva nevertheless.

The brightest period in the history of the city was in the 16th–17th centuries when lively transit trade passed through the city. Intentions of the Swedish government to turn Narva into the second Swedish capital speak about the importance of the city as a trading hub at the end of the 17th century. Also the 19th century was favourable to the development of Narva when the city became the centre of textile industry for northwestern Russia. In the course of numerous wars and fires the city of Narva has burnt down several times, but it has always risen from ashes and fast recovered thanks to its geographic location.

During and after World War II the population of Narva was fully replaced. In 1944 Narva was a front-line city for six months and all residents left it during that period. Most residential areas had badly suffered in air raids and shelling by the artillery, and in order to prevent the return of the previous residents after

◁ **Hermann Castle and bronze lion honoring Charles XII of Sweden**

◁ **Alexander Church, Narva**

Workers' tenements at the industrial Kreenholm settlement △

the war what remained of them was blasted, including practically all the former baroque old city. The present population of Narva is mainly made up of immigrants from Russian areas adjacent to Estonia and their descendants. The closest Russian metropolis, St Petersburg, lies only 150 kilometres from Narva.

So present-day Narva mainly dates from the post-war period with only a few houses going back to earlier periods – a few dwellings, the historical town hall and fragments of the belt of bastions surrounding the castle. The biggest ecclesiastic building in Estonia, the **Alexander Church of Narva** is still waiting for its restoration work to begin. The **Narva Castle** with its Pikk Hermann Tower was already restored in the Soviet period. It has a display on the history of Narva. The Castle Park and the former Victoria Bastion with the Pimeaed (Dark Garden) park are some of the favourite places where residents of Narva like to go for a walk. As also the Ivangorod Castle has been restored on the eastern bank of the Narva River, a unique

sight opens from the bridge crossing the Narva – two castles and two cultures in their centuries-old opposition, whose present and future can only be in equal respect of each other.

Besides the castle, also the historical **Kreenholm suburb** is worth seeing in Narva. It is mainly built up with late 19th century industrial buildings in the Historical style, making up the settlement of a huge textile mill. The Kreenholm factories were among the biggest of the kind in Europe with 10,000 employees before World War I. Even today the Kreenholm mill is the biggest employer in the city.

The name Kreenholm originally comes from the Swedish name of a Narva River island, Grönholm (Green Island). Earlier on it used to divide the river into two branches, with falls on both the branches. The **Narva Falls** were once regarded as one of the mightiest in Europe. With the construction of a hydroelectric power plant in the 1950s the river was conducted into a new channel and so the ledges and canyons of the falls are mostly dry today.

Oil-shaled fuelled Balti Power Plant ▽

Kuremäe Nunnery

The idyllic peace of the Pühtitsa Nunnery of the Assumption of the Virgin at Kuremäe is in sharp contrast with the mining areas. The flow of time is different there and even the people have different looks. The Orthodox Pühtitsa Nunnery is relatively new, established in 1892–95.

There are various legends about the revelations of Kuremäe. It is said that in the 16th century the Virgin appeared to an Estonian herdsman, and slightly later villagers found a large icon of the Assumption of the Virgin decorated with silver and pearls under a big oak. A small wooden chapel was put up at the spot, thus laying the basis to the cult of the Holy Hill. In the following centuries, the Kuremäe holy site was not widely known.

The imposing nunnery at Kuremäe was finally built in the Russification period at the end of the 19th century, when also the Orthodox Church was harnessed to that purpose. Today Kuremäe is an important centre of the Orthodox faith, being subordinated directly to Alexy II, the Patriarch of Moscow and All Russia. For forty years now the nunnery has lived under the guidance of Igumenya Varvara II.

The design of the general layout of the monastery and of the structures in the Old Russian style was by Professor Mikhail Preobrazhensky of the St Petersburg Academy of Arts. The complex has numerous buildings of various functions, all erected with the purpose of creating an integral ensemble: the nuns' dwellings, the winter church-canteen, the hospital, the Cathedral of the Assumption of the Virgin, the belfry, the Holy Gate, a school, a hotel, etc. The most important structure in the complex is the Uspensky (Assumption of the Virgin) Church, built in 1908–10 with five cupolas in a style imitating the ecclesiastic architecture of the Moscow-Yaroslavl school. The three-aisled church has three altars, a magnificent carved pine iconostasis and several rare frescos. The holiest relic is the icon of the Assumption of the Virgin of Jesus surrounded by Apostles and angels holding her mother's soul. There is room for 1,200 people in the cathedral.

Attached to the nunnery is a small auxiliary farm (cattle sheds, greenhouses, vegetable gardens). It is characteristic for the nuns to build large piles of firewood of logs laid in the fashion of haystacks. Although it is not a duty of the nunnery to serve visitors it is possible to agree on guiding services and the gates of the nunnery are generally open to everyone.

West Estonia

Saaremaa

Saaremaa (Island Land) is the biggest of Estonia's nearly 1,500 islands. To get to Saaremaa you have to board a ferry to cross the 8-kilometer-wide Suur Väin (Big Strait) and drive through Muhu Island. Saaremaa has a territory of 2,673 sq km, roughly equal with the Fyn Island of Denmark (2,985 sq km) and Saaremaa's historical neighbour, Sweden's Gotland Island (2,959 sq km). There are many similar features in the nature of Gotland and Saaremaa, mainly due to their common geological bedrock, Silurian limestone. So juniper stands on thin soils over the limestone bedrock and dry-stone walls built of stones picked from fields during their cultivation are characteristic of both the islands. There are nearly 600 smaller islands, islets or reefs around Saaremaa.

Saare County, comprising the islands of Saaremaa and Muhu, is one of the most highly valued holiday regions in the country. Recently many people from Estonia's northern neighbour, Finland, have discovered its charm and settled there, turning many old farms into beautiful summer homes. Saaremaa is characterised by juniper groves, picturesque village houses with thatch roofs and dry-stone walls, medieval churches and the developing resort town of Kuressaare.

◁ **Windmills at Angla**
▽ **Väike väin (Little Strait) causeway**

Kuressaare fortress and espiscopal castle

Kuressaare

Kuressaare, the capital of Saaremaa, developed in the 14th century around a bishop's castle built on the southern shore of the island. The place was granted a city charter in 1563 by Duke Magnus, brother of the king of Denmark, the then ruler of the island. Kuressaare's medieval name was *arx aquilla* (the Eagle's Castle), which gave it the old German name of Arensburg.

The massive keep with one gate and two towers built of dolomite ashlars was completed at the beginning of the 15th century. The perimeter wall with defence towers and bastions was built later and so was the powerful moat. Today the Kuressaare bishop's castle is the best-preserved medieval defence structure in Estonia. Restoration work of the castle, however, is going on despite that.

The castle houses the Saaremaa Museum, the castle grounds serving as the place for popular festivals, concerts and open-air performances. The castle is surrounded by a well-kept park of more than 150 years old, featuring a restored resort hall (Kursaal) and bandstand.

Kuressaare's baroque old town has the appearance it received by the end of the 17th century. The most outstanding buildings at the central square are the town hall, weigh house and several well-preserved dwelling houses. The singular weigh house with stepped gables is the only building of that function surviving in Estonia. The Kudjape cemetery at the edge of the town has several beautiful classical chapels.

Today Kuressaare is a small town of about 16,000 inhabitants. In the early 19th century it became known as a seaside resort where local sea mud was used for treatment. After the reestablishment of Estonian independence Kuressaare's resort economy is once again on the rising trend. Several new modern spas have been erected, with their clients mainly coming from Finland and other Nordic countries.

◁ **Town Hall**
◁ **Corner of Kuressaare's old town**
▽ **Central Square in Kuressaare**

Georg Ots Spa Hotel △

Marina ▽

Lake Kaali

A sight of international importance in Saaremaa is **Lake Kaali**, actually a meteorite crater with several other craters in its vicinity, all within about twenty kilometres from Kuressaare. Slightly more than 200 meteorite craters are known in the world and five or six of them are in Estonia thanks to the country having been so thoroughly studied. True enough, some of them are at the bottom of the sea or deep under the ground.

The meteoritic origin of the Kaali craters was proven in 1937 when fragments of an iron meteorite were found there. Scientists believe that the original mass of the meteorite could have been 1,000 tonnes and the speed at its contact with the ground as it fell from the east has been estimated at up to 20 kilometres per second. The main crater measures up to 110 meters across and is 16 metres deep. The crater with the lake at the bottom is surrounded with a bank 3–7 meters high consisting of soil torn up when the meteorite exploded. Layers of dolomite thrown into an upright position as a result of the blast are exposed on the inside of the crater. Besides the main crater there are eight further craters in the neighbourhood, measuring from 12-40 meters across and 1-4 metres deep.

In the 7th–6th centuries AD there was a fortified settlement on the northeastern side of the main crater. Debates about the age of the craters have been going on for decades. For a long time the prevailing opinion was that the meteorite fell about 2,700 years ago but now scientists seem to have agreed that it occurred around 1500 BC. The late Lennart Meri, a writer who later became the Estonian president, serving two terms of office in 1992–2001, has developed a whole theory about effects of the Kaali meteorite blast on the self-awareness of the people of Saaremaa and the whole northern Europe. Indeed, the meteorite plunging down to the ground like a hot ball of fire, and the explosion at its touchdown must have been a real shock to anyone witnessing it.

A small museum is open at Kaali to give an idea of the craters and the protected area around them.

Lake Kaali in a meteorite impact crater ▽

Vilsandi National Park

The present Vilsandi National Park comprises the island of Vilsandi off the northwestern coast of Saaremaa along with the surrounding sea, comprising some 160 islets and reefs, plus some coastal areas on Saaremaa. The total area of the National Park is nearly 180 square kilometres, the sea making up more than half of the total.

The history of the Park goes back to 1910 when the Vaika bird sanctuary was established. The first nature reserve in Estonia, it was born on the initiative of the Vilsandi lighthouse keeper Artur Toom and with the support of the Riga Society of Naturalists. A few years later, in 1913, the Saaremaa Naturalist Society was established, one of the first regional nature protection organisations in Estonia. Its founder, A Khrebtov, drew up and sent out a thorough circular on natural protection – the first appeal of this kind in the then Russian empire. Vilsandi received the status of National Park in 1993. The aim of the park is to protect coastal landscapes and the sea as well as to preserve ecosystems in which birds play a major role. About 250 species of breeding birds have been registered in the park, the most numerous species being the eider. Other common birds in Vilsandi are the goosander, the scaup, the mallard and the great black-backed gull. Plant species registered in the National Park total nearly 520, one third of all those found in Estonia. The island of Nootamaa, the westernmost point of Estonia, has 132 plant species. A wonderful view of the neighbouring islets and the sea opens from the

1809 Vilsandi lighthouse. Vilsandi's stony western shore is remarkable because of the fact that it consists of reefs formed more than 400 million years ago. Who cannot get to the island, can nevertheless get an exhaustive overview of the values of the National Park at the Loona Manor near Kihelkonna, the seat of the Park administration. There is also a guesthouse at Loona.

Valjala

The main sights at Valjala, once the most important centre on the island, are an old stronghold and a church. The **Valjala stronghold** (maalinn) was one of the biggest and strongest such sites in Estonia. It stands on a hill with the banks along its perimeter built of limestone slabs and earth. The stronghold is oval in its ground plan, measuring 120 meters long from the southwest to the northeast and 110 meters across. The ramparts are 5–8 meters high on the outside and 3–6 meters on the inside. Valjala's surrender to the crusaders in 1227 marked the end of the ancient's Estonians' resistance to foreign conquerors. The surrendered defenders were baptised immediately, and the water for baptism was apparently drawn from the well within the grounds of the stronghold. Lined with limestone slabs, it survives until the present.

Valjala Church is apparently the oldest surviving stone church in Estonia. It is believed that its construction started in the 13th century, soon after the surrender of the Valjala stronghold. Like most other Saaremaa churches the church in Valjala originally had no steeple, as in accordance with the rules of the Cistercian Order that operated in Old Livonia churches simultaneously had to be defence structures with thick walls and narrow windows placed high in the walls. The church was given a steeple only in the 17th century. Valjala Church combines Romanesque and Gothic traits. All the three round-arch portals are in the Romanesque style. The eastern portal with rich decorations is particularly stately, with a writhing plant ornamentation adorning the arch. The 1270 baptismal font is regarded as one of the most notable stone carvings in the Baltic countries.

Prehistoric Valjala stronghold

▽ St Martin's, Valjala

Karja

Karja Church is regarded as one of the most interesting country churches in Estonia. Built in the 13th—14th centuries, it has come down to our days in an almost unaltered shape, the only later addition being a southern hall added to the medieval structure, apparently in the 18th century.

The architecture of the church is extremely simple — a two-bay body, choir and vestry. There is no steeple. All the doors of Karja Church could be closed by means of crossbeams — here like everywhere else in medieval Saaremaa the house of god also served as a fortification. A room with a fireplace above the vaults of the vestry proves that refuge was sought between the walls of the church during wars and that it could have been offered also to pilgrims.

The church is valuable above all thanks to its sculptured décor. The portals, corbels and bosses are all decorated with masterly carvings of High Gothic form. Wall paintings from the period of construction survive in the choir. Magic signs once meant to ward off evil spirits such as the pentagram and triskele appear on the vaults of the choir. The church has a medieval baptismal font from the 14th century and a small altar crucifix from the late 15th century.

The cliff at Panga △

△ Windmill hill at Angla

Muhu

Muhu, the second largest island in Estonia (200 sq km) has been linked to Saaremaa by causeway for more than a hundred years now. The defining features of landscape are the level limestone bedrock that forms low hillocks, as well as a coastal bluff along the northern shore. There are many juniper stands on alvars where the plant cover is rich in different species.

Villages in Muhu stand out with their spick-and-span households and flower gardens. Muhu people have always loved bright colours and attractive patterns, which are also reflected in their traditional dress and in the Muhu people's special handicraft skills. Characteristic of the West-Estonian islands is a type of village called *sumbküla*, where the farms are located around a central village green without a clear plan, surrounded with fields and pastures. One of the most picturesque examples is the charming **Koguva Village**, which is wholly protected architecturally. The houses in Koguva are mainly from the period 1880–1920. The oldest buildings in the village are storehouses, some of them built as early as the 18th century. Side by side with the versatility of buildings, Koguva is striking by the integrity of its village ensemble with winding and cross-crossing village streets and breast-high dry-stone walls lining them. The stones, of which the walls were laid starting from the 17th century, were collected from the fields that were particularly stony in these parts. Besides farming, fishing played an important role in the islanders' life. Old boats on the dry-stone walls speak about the coastal people's cult of the sea – the boats were laid to rest on the dry-stone walls or were burnt in Midsummer Night bonfires.

Koguva Museum △
Young musicians in traditional Muhu dress △
Koguva. Village street ▽

 Pädaste Hotel △

◁ **The cliff at Üügu**

The Muhu Museum in Koguva provides a deeper insight into rural architecture and life.

Liiva in the middle of the island has an outstanding architectural monument – the **Muhu Church**, built at the end of the 13th century. From the outside, the church of monumental proportions looks stern. Adjoining the single-aisle two-bay main body of the church is a considerably narrower and lower choir with a singular quadrangular apse at its end. The peculiar tripartite composition of the building lends it a beautiful rhythm. The only architectural accents in the outward appearance are carved portals. The stylish early Gothic tracery of the windows has been mentioned to draw on West-European examples. The few and narrow windows, the narrow wall stairs leading up to the vaults and slots for the fastening of a crossbeam hint that the building has earlier been used as a defensive structure. It is worthwhile to look for trapeze-shaped gravestones with pagan symbols, dated to the 12th–13th centuries both in the church and in the churchyard. On the basis of the grave slabs and other archaeological finds there are reasons to believe that the church was built in an ancient Muhu people's holy site.

Close to the causeway linking Muhu with Saaremaa is the **Muhu stronghold** (maalinn) where the last battle of the Saare people against the united forces of the Knights of the Sword (*Fratres milicie Christi*) took place in 1227.

Pädaste Hall ▽

◁ **St Catherine's of Muhu**

△ **Heltermaa ferry port**

Hiiumaa

Hiiumaa (the Land of Giants), the second biggest Estonian island after Saaremaa, is situated farther from the mainland than its bigger neighbour. The nearest point to the mainland is 22 kilometres away and it takes nearly one and a half hours to cross the distance on a ferry. The coast of the island is shallow, the depth of the sea growing rather slowly, and there are numerous islets close to the shore. Northwest of Hiiumaa lie the notorious Neckmansgrund shoals on which dozens of ships have perished in olden days and about which numerous legends of false lighthouses and piracy have come down to our days. The settlement on Hiiumaa mainly clings to the coasts, with the interior of the island largely covered with marshes and forests. In Estonia Hiiumaa is mainly known by the peculiar humour of its inhabitants. As usual in the case of neighbours, friendly jokes about Saaremaa islanders are particularly frequent.

◁ **Kõpu Lighthouse**

Suuremõisa

Suuremõisa is the location of one of the most beautiful baroque manor complexes in Estonia. The history of the manor goes back to the 16th century, but the manor hall standing today was built in 1755–60. Originally the hall had 64 rooms. The most outstanding features include baroque balustrades in the hall and other carved wooden décor, the ceiling piece in the former dining hall, a secret door leading through a cupboard and a support wall, a vaulted cellar with sturdy pillars, large black kitchens with smoke hoods and the double ceiling of the attic, reportedly used to hide smuggled goods. Surrounding the manor hall is a 200-year-old park in the English style. Since 1796 until its expropriation in 1919 the manor hall belonged to the Baltic-German family of the von Ungern-Sternbergs, who ruled from there its lands making up a large part of the island. Of the landlords, Otto Reinhold Ludwig von Ungern-Stenberg (1744–1811) acquired a peculiar fame – there were rumours that he led ships aground on the Neckmansgrund shoals by means of false lights. The wrecked ships were then plundered, which explains the reason for the numerous hideouts between the ceilings in the manor hall. Another fact adding credibility to the rumours was that the lord was actually involved in rescue at sea, which in those times was a paid job. Although no cases of piracy could ever be proven, the man died deported to Siberia after all, for killing a Swedish skipper in his office in a fit of rage in 1802.

Today a basic school and a technical school work in Suuremõisa Hall.

Kassari

Although linked to Hiiumaa with causeways, **Kassari** is a separate island and worth a visit. The main axis of the island is a ridge up to 15 meters high, from where views open here and there of the Väinameri Sea over the junipers. In clear weather you can see the offshore islets and distant peninsulas as well as the coast of Saaremaa. From the Orjaku observation tower to which there is a sign-posted nature trail, the whole Käina Bay, a bird sanctuary overgrown with reeds, is like on the palm of your hand.

Sääre tirp at the southern end of Kassari is a narrow spit reaching one and a half kilo-metres into the sea, the configuration of the end of the spit changing location according to whims of the sea. There is a folk tale that the Hiiumaa giant Leiger once carried the stones the spit is made of into the sea, so it would be simpler for his brother Tõll, who lived in Saaremaa, to come visiting.

Kassari is highly valued as a summer place, particularly among artists and people of letters. One confirmation of the fact is the **house museum of Aino Kallas** (1878–1956), an Estonian-Finnish writer.

Kõpu

That long peninsula is the geological cradle of the whole island – the hill where the lighthouse now stands, 68 metres above sea level, first emerged from the sea as a little islet about 10,000 years ago. Kõpu was then an isolated bit of dry land in the midst of the sea with the mainland nearly 80 kilometres away. Kõpu offers you the opportunity of being alone with the sea but you can also venture inland to see the Kõpu Lighthouse. The massive quadrangular structure of boulders and limestone supported by four buttresses, one the oldest operating sea signs in the Baltic, is 36 meters high, with the light blinking at nearly 103 meters above sea level. Among constantly operating lighthouses, Kõpu is the third oldest in the world.

Construction of the lighthouse started in the first decade of the 16th century, apparently around 1504. Kõpu became a real lighthouse only in 1649 when a wooden staircase was built outside the structure and a grill for the burning of coals and wood was hauled up to the top. It consumed 800–1000 fathoms of firewood a year. Premises for the crew and steps were cut into the originally solid interior in 1810.

An extensive panorama of the whole peninsula with its forests and the sea beyond opens from the observation platform of the lighthouse.

For a tour of the Kõpu hills there is a 1.5 kilometre nature trail at Rebastemäe. The rumble of the sea does not leave the visitor anywhere in Kõpu. At the upper head of Ristna, a windsurfers' paradise, the waves roll in with all their might.

Reigi Church △
Kärdla. Central Square ▷
Soera Farm Museum ▽

Vormsi

Vormsi, the fourth biggest Estonian island (93 sq km) can be reached by ferry from Rohuküla to Sviby. In the winter an ice track is opened along the same route, marked by wooden stakes and warning signs (keep the doors so they can be opened easily, recommended speed 40 – 70 km per hour). There

are periods when the island is cut off from the mainland for several weeks running, particularly in the spring when the ice starts breaking up and can no longer be trusted but is still too strong for the navigation season to start.

Vormsi (Ormsö in Swedish) is a low island that started rising from the sea about 3,000 years ago. Many of its place names hark back to times when the local language was Swedish. Cape Rumpo and the headlands of Austurgrunne and Rälbyklubba stretch far out into the sea. The small Väike-Tjuka Island can be reached on foot. Even in the interior of the island we meet signs of the sea everywhere. In the Fällarna forest the traveller finds the Hoitberg coral reef – a hangover from the Silurian Sea when the present location of Estonia was situated somewhere in a warm tropical sea. Hullo Bay (Hulloviken) continues deep inland as Lake Prästviken – a former bay of the sea that is now growing over. There are large erratic boulders in several parts of the island, signs of the carrying capacity of the glaciers.

The permanent population of the island amounts to about 330, mostly settlers from the mainland. The earlier Swedish community (2,400 Swedish-speaking residents in 1934) left during World War II to settle in Sweden.

The Swedish settlement of the island dated back to the 13th century and has left a characteristic legacy also in addition to place names. A church dedicated to St Olaf (the 11th century canonised King Olaf II Haraldsson of Norway) attracts attention slightly away from Hullo, the central settlement of the island. The choir of the church was completed in the early 14th century and its main body in 1632. The church has no steeple, and there is a figure of St Olaf in a niche in the outer wall.

Next to the church is the world's biggest cemetery featuring solar crosses. Such solar crosses, of which there are more than 300, were in use in the 17th–20th centuries. In all likelihood each family on the island had its family sign used to mark fishing gear and household appliances. The same signs were also used on the crosses. As a result more information is recorded on the crosses by means of the signs than by means of letters. It is remarkable that the sandstone of which the crosses were made is not found on Vormsi. It is therefore believed that the stone to make the crosses was brought from Gotland, from where it was exported also to Riga, St Petersburg and Tallinn.

Haapsalu

A peaceful small town of 12,000 inhabitants, Haapsalu attracts those who love narrow streets, old wooden houses, views of the sea, quiet walks and the opportunity to be alone with one's thoughts.

The sea surrounds Haapsalu on three sides. From the old part of the town any street leads to the sea after just a few minutes' walk. Haapsalu has risen around a 13th century **bishop's castle**, which is still the main attraction of the town. The oldest buildings in the castle are the so-called small fortress and a single-aisle cathedral church, to which a round baptismal chapel was annexed in the 14th century. The castle with the grounds within its walls is well preserved and is used as an arena for summer open-air performances and other activities.

On full moon nights in August large crowds gather in the castle grounds to witness the appearance of the White Lady of Haapsalu. Characteristically of old castles the White Lady is naturally just a legend.

In the times of the bishops the canons, of course, had to lead ascetic and modest lives. Legend has it that one of the canons had nevertheless brought into the castle a young girl dressed as a choirboy. The secret soon came to light and it was decided to bury the young girl alive in a wall of the castle

▽ **Ruins of the Haapsalu bishop's castle and St Nicholas's Cathedral**

that was being built at the time. As for the sinful canon, he was locked into the castle's prison where he eventually died of hunger. Cries could be long heard from the hollow in the wall. A couple of times every year at full moon the sad figure of the lady appears in a window of the baptismal chapel. In the Middle Ages the small fortress contained the living quarters and workrooms of the bishop, the canons and the monks. It was also the seat of the Cathedral School (Toomkool), one of the oldest schools in Estonia first mentioned in 1280.

The small fortress was extended during the centuries until the 38-metre watchtower was completed in the 15th century. Splendid views of the town open from its top. Two outer wards were built next to the small fortress in the 14th–16th centuries and the 803-meter-long perimeter wall was completed. Today the castle houses a museum providing an overview of the history of the castle. A noteworthy collection of weapons from the 15th and 16th centuries is on display.

Haapsalu became famous as a seaside resort when the remedial properties of the local sea mud were discovered and it was taken into use for curative purposes at the beginning of the 19th century. The first mud-bath treatment facility was opened in 1825 and medical institutions using local mud have operated in the town ever since then. The resort achieved the peak of its first fame at the beginning of the 20th century when the town received a railway link with Tallinn and St Petersburg. Parks and promenades, summerhouses and entertainment institutions were built. An elegant resort hall (Kursaal) with intricate wooden decorations surviving in the original shape today was completed in 1898. Holidaymakers arrived in Haapsalu even from St Petersburg. An awning 216 meters long was built over the platform at the railway station for the reception of the Tsar and his family, so Their Excellencies would not get wet in case of a shower.

Contrary to the Russian practice of using standard designs for railway stations, an original design was commissioned for the station in Haapsalu. The building consists of two parts, the Passenger Hall and the Imperial Pavilion linked by an awning. The railway station in the Historical style has become one of the symbols of Haapsalu. Rail traffic on the Tallinn-Haapsalu route has today been ousted by motor traffic and the station platform is usually deserted. The railway station now serves as the railway museum and the tourist information centre. In addition to the family of the tsar also the famous Russian composer Pyotr Tchaikovsky, the painter Nikolai Roerich and other prominent people have rested in Haapsalu.

Swedish royalty have visited Haapsalu as well. Although the town was not situated in the Estonian Swedes' settlement area, Haapsalu was still the most important town for the Swedes of Noarootsi and Vormsi. There is a special Estonian Swedes' museum in

◁ **Sundial**
◁ **Tchaikovsky's bench**

98

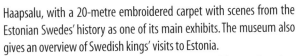

Haapsalu, with a 20-metre embroidered carpet with scenes from the Estonian Swedes' history as one of its main exhibits. The museum also gives an overview of Swedish kings' visits to Estonia.

Today Haapsalu is known above all as a resort town, with several modern rehabilitation centres and spas opened in it and valued particularly by Nordic visitors.

At the time of completion, the 216-metre platform of Haapsalu's railway station was the longest in northern Europe

▽

Matsalu National Park

Matsalu is known above all as a bird sanctuary. It has splendid habitats for different species of birds in the form of coastal pastures, reed beds, water meadows and sea islands in the mouth of the Kasari River, of which Matsalu Bay is an extension. Matsalu is also an important stopover place for migratory birds, whose route takes them further from Matsalu to the tundra areas of the White Sea. Hundreds of thousands of migratory birds a year stop in Matsalu, the most numerous among them being swans, geese, barnacle geese, ducks, etc.

A hundred and fifty-seven species of breeding and 280 species of migratory birds have been registered in the National Park. The Park's main activity is the study of birds, preservation of their living and stopover places, which also means taking care of the coastal pastures so they won't grow over with bushes. Winter reed cutting on top of the ice is done to make for more versatile nesting opportunities for

Penijõe Hall, office of the National Park △

the birds and to supply the raw material for the characteristic Lääne County thatched roofs.

There are five nature trails for bird watchers and six bird observation towers in the Park. The administration and museum of the National Park are situated in the newly renovated Penijõe Hall, where one can

◁ Kasari River

Water meadow of the Kasari in early spring ▽

View from the Lihula fort hill △
Lihula Hall △

get a good overview of the nature in the whole area, above all its bird life. It is also possible to buy boat trips through the reeds and on Matsalu Bay. The landscape in the vicinity of Matsalu Bay is characteristically level and open. Here and there on the southern bank limestone bluffs rise above the surrounding ground, marking the higher parts of the West-Estonian Clint. The limestone outcrops continue in the westerly

direction with the Muhu and Saaremaa Clints and end with the Gotland Clint in Sweden.

A stone fortress was built instead of an ancient Estonians' stronghold on the Lihula limestone elevation in the 13th century. Ruins of the **Lihula Castle** have been recently conserved and a catapult has been built to give an idea of the former battles in Lihula's vicinity.

▽ Elk in a meadow

The beach in Pärnu ▷

Pärnu

For years already there is a ceremony at the beginning of summer, by which Tallinn symbolically hands over the title of capital to Pärnu, the summer capital, and takes it back again in the autumn.

The city sprang up at the head of a bay where the Pärnu River, the longest in Estonia, falls into the sea. The Pärnu River basin has been an old settlement area, where the river served as the main traffic artery. Traces of Estonia's oldest settlement site (about 11,000 years old) have been found at Pulli on the lower reaches of the Pärnu.

The fact that Pärnu was once a medieval Hanseatic city can only be surmised by a few buildings in the old town – the **Red Tower** (15th century), the only defence tower remaining of the medieval town wall, a stretch of moat and the **Tallinn Gate**, the only 17th century rampart gate extant in the Baltic countries. An open-air stage has found a suitable location on a former bastion in the neighbourhood of the half-filled moat. The town has beautiful examples of architecture in baroque (**St Elizabeth's** and **St Catherine's** churches, 18th century), Classical (**Town Hall**, 1797), Historical (**Bristol Hotel**) and Art Nouveau (Ammende Villa). The most outstanding new construction projects in Pärnu are the study building of Tartu University's **Pärnu College** and the seashell-inspired **Concert House**.

The basis for the status of the summer capital is the kilometre-long Pärnu bathing beach, where the water is warm and the slope gentle. A bathing establishment opened in 1838 laid the basis to Parnu's fame as a seaside resort. The parks and avenues were mostly laid out at the end of the 19th century. To prevent shifting sands from obstructing the sea-lane there are stone piers about two kilometres long to protect the Pärnu River mouth. Built in 1864, they soon became a favourite outing place for the townspeople.

One of the high periods in the life of the green holiday resort was in the 1930s when a mushroom-shaped functionalist **Rannakohvik** (Bach Café) with a balcony and terraces as well as the stylish **Rannahotell** (Beach Hotel) were built on the beach. Both the buildings by the local architect Olev Siinmaa have remained symbols of the Pärnu resort until today.

In the summer there are days when the number of visitors surpasses that of Pärnu's own population. It is then a problem to book a time to play tennis in a court in the coastal park and the numerous yachtsmen arriving at the marina do not hurry to leave after stocking up. In the summer the concert and art venues of the town spring to new life. An international festival of anthropological films, a musical festival initiated decades ago by the famous violinist David Oistrakh, and in the recent years also the master courses for conductors by the world-famous orchestra leader Neeme Järvi are some of the traditional events of a Pärnu summer.

In addition to beach holidays in the summer Pärnu offers opportunities of treatment and rest the year round. The town boasts about ten rehabilitation and treatment centres and spas.

Paradise and Aquatic Park of Spa Hotel Tervis ▽

Kihnu

Kihnu Island (16.4 sq km) lies in the Gulf of Riga 10.5 kilometres from the mainland. It is unique among Estonian Baltic Sea islands, as there are many more old features in the everyday life, traditions and dress of its residents than elsewhere, providing the ground to speak about an independent Kihnu cultural space. The individuality is mainly due to the island's relative isolation, as a result of which its old-established population of up to 1,300 has developed over the centuries with little influence from the mainland. Today it is no longer a problem to get to the island as there is both a boat line and air link, and the welfare of the Kihnu people does not depend on the sea alone any more – the world has come to Kihnu and the other way round. The individuality of Kihnu has become an asset but its preservation is no longer automatically granted and so needs protection. This need has been recognised on the highest level: UNESCO has declared the Kihnu cultural space intangible and spiritual heritage of humanity.

Today's Kihnu is a combination persisting thanks to strong traditions and moderate changes in them. The local dialect still lives on in Kihnu today and is even taught at the island's school. Nowhere else in Estonia are traditional costumes worn so widely as Kihnu women do it. Kihnu customs, particularly weddings, are deeply individual and

Midsummer Night bonfire

could be even tiring to those coming from the mainland – the festivities last for at least three days. Although the former important men's activities, sailing and sealing, have remained in the past, the sea still provides livelihood. Fishing is still a respectable occupation and for many men it is the only opportunity to earn a living. Kihnu women, who actually run the whole household on the island, are very brave. They can do all the men's work, and they often have to actually stand in for men, even at sea. In some spheres they have not succeeded, however – so the self-taught Kihnu naïve painters have all been men. Their most famous works, mainly to themes of the sea and navigation, have ended up in galleries and museums overseas, and a good selection of their pictures is on display also at the **Kihnu Museum**.

Today, the island's four villages are home to about 560 people, who have to get accustomed to the ever growing number of inquisitive visitors. Besides the museum, Kihnu has a church and a communal government, a modern community centre, as well as several farms providing accommodation and meals for the visitors.

Ruhnu

Kihnu's next-door neighbour in the Gulf of Riga is the lonely **Ruhnu** (Swedish: Runö) Island (11.9 sq km). When the 300-strong indigenous Swedish-speaking population of Ruhnu left for Sweden in 1944 to escape Soviet occupation, the island remained almost deserted. Later people have settled there from Kihnu as well as from the mainland.

There have been better and worse times in the life of the island after the war, and the population has become stabilised at about 60. Yet the island has its own communal government, port, post office, lighthouse, border guard post, medical service, airport and weather station. There are as many as five farms providing accommodation.

Connection with Ruhnu is via Kuressaare, but both the summer boat service and the round-the-year air link have a large proportion of the indefinite in them. The eastern duneland part of Ruhnu is higher, rising to 28 meters above sea level. A metal lighthouse erected in 1877 stands there. The layout of the only settlement in the middle of the island is archaic, without any clear plan. There are a counted few houses going back to times of the Swedes, most having been later rebuilt, but at the northern edge of the village there are two churches standing side by side to attract your attention.

St Magdalene's wooden church of Ruhnu is the oldest extant wooden building in Estonia, completed in 1644. The present altar and pulpit date from 1855. Family signs and other symbolic carvings can be seen on the ends of the pews.

The new granite church with a wooden steeple was built next to the old one in 1912. Attached to the churches is a cemetery with peculiar archaic wooden crosses.

◁ Ruhnu's old wooden church and new stone church

▽ Interior of wooden church, with family signs cut into the end posts of pews

Soomaa National Park

After the bogs and marshy forests intersected by a dense network of rivers and streams were brought under the administration of a national park in 1993, the popularity of Soomaa has been steadily growing. A lot of it is certainly due to canoe trips, which have become so popular that there are days where up to a hundred boats are afloat on rivers of the National Park, although there could be room for many more. The duration of the trips can vary from a few hours to four to five days. As the road network is rather sparse in Soomaa and what roads there are often tend to be muddy, use of rivers as arteries of traffic has traditionally been quite common in the area.

In Soomaa it is possible to hear the silence of the primeval woods and to see the biggest inland inundations in Estonia. The causes of the periodical flooding are seemingly simply, although it is very difficult to forecast high water. Soomaa is a low and level area adjacent to the mostly cultivated Sakala highlands. On higher land the snow melts faster in the spring than in the more low-lying forests. So the situation arises where the rivers are unable to let all the melt water pass. The thickness of the snow cover and the depth to which the ground is frozen in the winter add nuances to the floods. There is a saying that there a five seasons in Soomaa – spring, summer, autumn, winter and high water. The water in Soomaa rivers can rise up to five meters above the summer low-water mark. In level areas the rivers rise beyond their banks and so the flood spreads out far into the forests. In some years the flooded area has been estimated to cover up to 150 sq km – it was over such a territory that the forests and bogs were covered with shallow water about one meter in depth.

The flooded area of Soomaa has attracted the attention of researchers since decades ago: for the naturalist the flooded meadows and forests are an interesting object of study, and ethnographers are keen to learn how the local people have become adapted to live with the floods, making them use a local water craft, *haabjas*, an aspen dugout, until the most recent times. The *haabjas* is made of one aspen trunk hollowed out with special adzes, the body of the boat being alternately moistened and dried, bent with various stakes and so in about a week of work the pod-shaped boat is ready to be launched. Although it looks rather frail, it is a surprisingly safe craft in the hands of an expert. In former days the *haabjas* was used on an equal footing with the horse in Soomaa, as their was no better assistant than the dugout when it came to saving hay from a drowning haystack. Soomaa's population has always been sparse and even today there are perhaps only a hundred people living in the 370 sq km territory of the National Park.

The Park visitor centre provides a movie program on Soomaa, accommodation, sauna, playgrounds for children and various routes for hikes. There is a separate nature trail to learn the habits of the beavers, where traces of the animal's activity can be studied.

PERÄJÄRV

South Estonia

Tartu

Tartu, the second biggest city in Estonia, is the most important centre in the south of the country. As a university town since 1632, Tartu has always been the centre of Estonia's spiritual life and it is difficult to overestimate Tartu's contribution to Estonian education, science and culture. Contrary to the rational and businesslike Tallinn, Tartu is cha-racterised by certain academic peace as for more than two centuries the university has been the focal point defining the pace of life in the city. Tartu is sometimes fondly called Emajõe Ateena, Athens of the Emajõgi, while the Russian name Yuryev and the German Dorpat have earlier been in official use. The **Emajõgi** (Mother River), the stream that flows through the city, is Estonia's biggest river. It is a historical waterway flowing at the bottom of a mighty primeval valley and its bed is the narrowest as it passes through Tartu. For this reason it was a point of crossing the river already in the period before bridges and a fortified settlement of the Estonians

◁ **Tartu University main building**

△ Ruins of medieval cathedral on Toome Hill,
◁ housing the University History Museum

was established there as early as the 5th–6th century AD. The first mention of the place in written sources was in connection with the conquest and burning of the fortification by Prince Yaroslav the Wise of Kiev in 1030. The city surrendered to the crusaders in 1224.

The historical heart of the city is **Toomemägi** (Toome Hill), the location of the ancient stronghold, which rises 30 meters above the surrounding terrain. Ruins of a 13th century cathedral survive on it. At the beginning of the 19th century the university library was built into the surviving choir of the magnificent Gothic brick structure; today it is in use as the **University History Museum**.

In fact, most of the structures on Toomemägi date from the 19th century, when several university buildings, such as the anatomical theatre and the observatory were put up there. Those taking a walk on Toomemägi will pass a monument to the best-known naturalist to have studied and lived in Tartu, Karl Ernst von Baer (1792–1876), a theoretician of evolution and discoverer of the ovum. It is at this monument that students in their colourful caps traditionally assemble on Walpurgis Night (April 30). Young members of the Estonian Student Society then scrub the bronze head of the venerable scientist clean with champagne and a sponge. At close quarters from Baer stands the monument to

◁ Monument to Karl Ernst von Baear

the first Estonian poet, Kristjan Jaak Peterson (1801–22), who died at the tender age of 21.

There are two footbridges on Toomemägi connecting its slopes – the **Angel's Bridge** (Inglisild) and the **Devil's Bridge** (Kuradisild). The Angel's Bride was completed in 1838 and bears the bas-relief portrait of the then rector of the university Georg Friedrich Parrot and the Latin text, *Otium reficit vires* – Rest Restores Strength.

The Devil's Bridge, whose name has been given in contrast to that of the Angel's Bridge, was built in 1913 to mark the tercentenary of the House of Romanov and is dedicated to the memory of Tsar Alexander I, who decided the reopening of the University in 1802.

The heart of modern Tartu is **Raekoja plats** (Town Hall Square). The 18th century Town Hall houses the city government. The Kissing Students fountain in front of the Town Hall has become a popular meeting place. The whole square is lined with stylish Early Classical buildings, including Tartu's own Tower of Pisa – a **slanting house** that once belonged to the famous field marshal Barclay de Tolly, governor-general of Finland and commander-in-chief of the Russian army in the Napoleonic wars. The whole of the old town of Tartu has been built in the marshy valley flat of the Emajögi, partly on wooden stakes. A pedestrian arch bridge (Kaarsild) links Raekoja Plats with the opposite side of the river.

Gustavus II Adolphus, founder of Tartu University ▷

▽ **Angel's Bridge on Toome Hill**

△ Town Hall

Kissing Students fountain in front of the Town Hall ▽

△ Rüütli tänav

Model of old Stone Bridge (1781–1941) next to the present footbridge across the Emajõgi ▽

Student corporation revelling in Raekoja plats

Tartu University main building △
University festive hall ▽

△ Statues of the Estonian writer Eduard Vilde and the Irish writer Oscar Wilde in front of Vilde Café

The **embankment** of the Emajõgi is a favourite place for walking. It has a monument to the author of the Estonian national epic *Kalevipoeg*, Friedrich Reinhold Kreutzwald, and a figure of Kalevipoeg himself has been erected as a monument to the victorious War of Independence.

In the city centre, sitting on a bench in front of the popular **Wilde Café** in the building of a printing press opened in 1766 there are two famous writers, the Estonian Eduard Vilde and the Irish author Oscar Wilde. In 2004 a copy of the sculpture of the two namesakes was erected in the Irish city of Galway to mark enlargement of the European Union.

Tartu's characteristic atmosphere is preserved in the historical **wooden suburbs** such as Karlova and Supilinn (Soup Town), where the streets are named after vegetables, as well as the so-called professors' quarter of Tähtvere. The city has numerous museums, several of them being centres of scientific research, such as the geology, zoology, ethnography and literary museums and the botanical gardens.

St John's of Tartu, decorated with hundreds of terra cotta figures ▽

Tartu University is the second oldest in the Baltic countries after Vilnius University. There is a monument to King Gustavus II Adolphus of Sweden at the back of the university main building marking the opening of the university in 1632. The university of the Swedish period wound up its activities when Swedish power in the country ended and was reopened in the Russian empire in 1802, after a break of more than a hundred years. Ever since then, the Classical main building with its six-columned portico designed by Johann Wilhelm Krause has been the heart and visual symbol of the university. Tartu University achieved world fame as a German-medium higher educational institution in the mid-19th century. Most great names in Estonian cultural history have studied there. The biologist Karl Ernst von Baer, the physiologist Alexander Schmidt, the astronomer Friedrich Georg Wilhelm Struve, the Nobel Prize winning chemist Wilhelm Ostwald and many other have worked there. Since 1919 the language of tuition at the university has been Estonian and it is still the leading higher educational institution in the country.

One of the most important sights in the old town is the 14th century **St John's Church** (Jaani kirik), decorated with unique terra cotta figures. Its restoration from damages caused in World War II is still going on.

St John's of Tartu ▷

Viljandi

The county seat of Viljandi is situated on the bank of a picturesque primeval valley, with the scenic long **Lake Viljandi** glistening at its bottom. There is an old popular song about an aged Viljandi boatman rowing on the lake and still remembering a young lady of his youth whom he had once taken across the water. "These beautiful blue eyes conquered my heart," go the lyrics.

The town itself, like many in Estonia, sprang up next to an old **Order Castle**. The natural conditions were very favourable for the building of a stronghold. On the promontory at the meeting point of two steep-sloped ravines protection against attackers was already insured by the relief. To further fortify the place it was only necessary to dig the moats that are still clearly visible in the outer ward and to build a strong defensive wall. A powerful stronghold of the Estonians, sieges to which were repeatedly mentioned in chronicles, had earlier occupied the site where the Knights of the Sword erected their stone fortress in 1224. Construction of the order castle lasted several centuries with intervals and the result was impressive. The system of fortifications covered three adjacent hills, the farthest and best-protected part being the keep, which was second in size in Livonia only to the castle of Riga. Sustaining damages in numerous conquests and sieges the order

▽ **Ruins of the Order Castle**

castle lost its military importance after the Livonian War in the late 16th century. The territory of the former castle is now known as **Lossimäed** (Castle Hills), one of the favourite haunts of both residents and visitors of the city, where open air performances and concerts take place in the summer.

A walk on the Castle Hills is almost unthinkable without crossing the **suspension bridge** (Rippsild) leading across a former moat from the ruins of the keep. The suspension bridge swaying to the rhythm of the walker's steps, the Castle Hills and Lake Viljandi together with the boatman yearning for beautiful blue eyes are all inseparable symbols of Viljandi.

A quiet area of wooden houses with peaceful streets and green parks laid out in a regular pattern makes up the oldest part of Viljandi. Characteristic of the town are numerous red brick public buildings mostly dating from the 19th century. The conspicuous old water tower, now nearly a hundred years old, has been turned into a café.

In the 1880s Viljandi was an important centre of the Estonian national movement. One of the most notable names in that period when the Estonians' national awareness became established was Carl Robert Jakobson (1841–1882) – author of novel school-books, promoter of agriculture, politician and journalist, who published an important national newspaper, Sakala, in Viljandi. Also Johann Köler (1826–1899), a pioneer of Estonian painting, studied in Viljandi. The town has a monument to General Johan Laidoner (1884–53). The commander-in-chief of the Estonian

Suspension bridge across former moat in the Castle Hills ▷

armed forces in the War of Independence was born near the town. Today Viljandi is a town of nearly 20,000 inhabitants that does not live on the past alone. The town has a professional theatre, Ugala, and a higher educational institution, the Academy of Culture. Events taking place in Viljandi are known far and wide. So the spring run around Lake Viljandi has taken place without a break since 1928. Like many athletes never skip a run, so also many members of the public are always present to cheer the competitors. The international Viljandi folk music festival every summer brings as many people into Estonia as there are residents.

Lake Peipsi

The fourth biggest fresh-water body in Europe, the twin Lakes of Peipsi and Pskov constitute Estonia's border with Russia. Peipsi is large enough to have its own system of currents, its own peculiarities of waves, and its own specific fishes, such as tint (sparling), rääbis (European lake whitefish), Peipsi siig (Peipsi lavaret). The ice cover of Lake Peipsi often plays tricks, building ramparts the height of multi-storeyed houses along the shore, which then take until early summer to melt.

The lake is relatively shallow, the deepest point being 15 meters in Lämmijärv, the narrow neck connecting the twins. The fierce Ice Battle took place in 1242 close to that place, where Alexander Nevsky, the Prince of Novgorod, defeated an army of the crusaders and stopped their further advance to the east.

The Peipsi shore, 175 kilometres on the Estonian side, is quite varied in character. The northern shore is a beautiful sandy beach. It is a an area in constant change, with the coastal bank retreating due to wind and wave action, river estuaries clogging up and the dunes growing in height. It is also a place where a phenomenon called the singing sands can be observed. It is believed that when a grain of sand rubs against another at a certain angle and a certain speed, the "singing" sound is herd. Grains of the singing sand are smoother and more streamlined than those of ordinary sand. In Europe singing sands are known in addition to North-Estonia's sandy beaches only in Ireland. The northern shore of Lake Peipsi has numerous camping sites and holiday places. There are few local inhabitants, but numerous holiday-makers in the summer.

Peipsi's western shore is mostly flat, sandy stretches being few and far between. At Kallaste the waves have modelled the sandstone bank into a bluff up to 11 meters in height. Extensive marshlands surround the estuary of the Emajõgi.

Estonian and Russian communities have long lived side by side on the western shore of Lake Peipsi. The old-established Peipsi Russians are Old Believers, who mainly settled there in the 17th century when Patriarch Nikon launched a reform of the Russian Orthodox Church. It led to sharp contradictions between the pro-renewal Orthodox and

Old Believers who found the nearest refuge from repressions and outlawry from lands to the west of Lake Peipsi. So Russian settlements sprang up at Mustvee, Kallaste, Raja, Varnja, Kolkja and Kasepää. The Old Believers have remained true to the principles of Russian Orthodoxy as it was formed in the tenth century. They use Old Slavonic in services and their baptisms are more archaic than those of the other Orthodox believers. There are about 15,000 Old Believers in Estonia today.

The life of Peipsi Russians has always been connected with the lake – fishing has provided livelihood to them and their households stand side by side along the lakeshore. Most of the villages lie so close to each other that the shore of Lake Peipsi often looks like one long village street. Onion, chicory and gherkin growing spread as a source of livelihood when it became possible to start marketing the produce in Tartu, Narva and St Petersburg. Vegetable growing is the inhabitants' main activity until today. Passing Old Believers' houses the daily life of the people is clearly in view – rows or *vobla*, roach, drying on strings in the yard and onion fields spreading at the back of the house. A fish and onion restaurant offering local specialities has been opened in Kolkja Village. The bigger towns on Lake Peipsi are Mustvee and Kallaste.

Winter fishing △

Old Believers' villages and chapel on Lake Peipsi

△ **Alatsksivi Hall**

Mustvee has sometimes been called the Estonian gherkin capital. Gherkin and cucumber growing was particularly profitable in Soviet times, when the produce could be marketed in Leningrad. Mustvee can also be regarded as a town of churches. Although the place only has 2,000 residents, it has four churches, including one of Old Believers, but in former times there were as many as seven of them. There is also an Old Believers' museum in Mustvee.

The best-known icon-painter of the Old Believers, Piomen Sofronov (1898–1973) was born at Tiheda a few kilometres south of Mustvee. He learned to paint on the shores of Lake Peipsi, but later lived and painted icons in various parts in Europe and the United States.

A short distance from the lake and the Russian settlement area is the Gothic Revival Alatskivi Hall, whose second youth hopefully lies ahead. The manor hall was designed and built by the owner, Arved von Nolcken, after his trip to Scotland in 1885, where the British royal residence of Balmoral left a strong impression on him. It is said the manor hall featuring several towers and turrets originally had 99 rooms. There was a beautiful rose garden behind the mansion and a park with sculptures around it. After the owners were forced to leave, it served as a school, border guard station, machine and tractor station and the office of a Soviet state farm. Now the manor hall is being turned into a holiday and cultural centre. The vicinity of Alatskivi is linked with one of the widest read Estonian poets, Juhan Liiv (1864–1913). The nearby Rupsi Village has a museum of Juhan Liiv and his brother Jakob, also a poet and writer.

Otepää hill fort △

Otepää and its Vicinity

Otepää, a small town of about 2,500 inhabitants, derives its name from the local prehistoric Karupea (Bear's Head, *Oti pää* in the vernacular) hill fort. Otepää has a special place in Estonia's history, because the blue, black and white flag of the Estonian Student

World Cup race in Nordic skiing in Otepää ▽

Society was consecrated at the Otepää parsonage in 1884. It later became the Estonian national flag. The first blue, black and white flag is still extant, safeguarded by the Society in Tartu. Tablets marking consecration of the flag decorate a wall of Otepää's church.

Today Otepää is known above all as a winter sports centre. Opening of a Tartu University sports centre at Kääriku, 10 kilometres from Otepää, laid the basis to it in the 1960s. Thanks to the varied relief of the area and snow cover that is usually thicker in Otepää than elsewhere in Estonia, the place is perfectly suitable to be a winter sports centre. In the last decade Otepää has proven itself as a venue of international Nordic skiing championship races and a place where some of the world's best skiers like to train. The ski stadium immediately outside the town draws large numbers of public to cheer the competitors making their last exertions before the finish. Most top-level Estonian skiers have studied at the Otepää skiing school.

Otepää is also a Mecca of amateur slalomists, snow boarders and Sunday skiers, for whom there are various services and winter events. The yearly Tartu Maraton race over a 60-kilometre cross-country track, to which the starting signal is given near Otepää, draws thousands of participants. From the distance it looks like a mighty human river winding its way up and down hillocks.

During the winter Golden Fish competition thousands of anglers attempt to catch a marked fish through holes bored in the ice. It is not easy to catch the Gold Fish and win the main prize, a car, but the event is very popular nevertheless – everyone, after all, wins a day in the open air.

There are dozens of places offering accommodation, including farmhouses, in the vicinity of Otepää, all of them providing also various open-air activities.

The rolling landscape of green hills alternating with mirror lakes, a nature park and exciting nature trails are bringing more and more holidaymakers to Otepää also in the summer.

The scenic **Lake Pühajärv** (Holy Lake) with five islands and a creeky shore lies at close quarters from Otepää. According to tradition it has received its name from a sacred oak growing close to its shore. Nearly every farm around the lake has hosted painters and other artistic people. During his visit to Estonia in 1991 the 14th Dalai Lama Tenzin Gyatso gave his blessing to Lake Pühajärv.

The **Leigo** Farm lies within twenty kilometres from Otepää. For a number of years already its dammed-up lakes are the scene of exhilarating open airs concerts on mellow August nights. High-level performers recite at the concerts attracting thousands of people to watch a majestic spectacle of fire and music as the sun falls below the horizon.

Lake Kääriku

Typical South Estonian landscape △

Lake music concert at Leigo ▽

Karula National Park

The **Karula National Park** is situated away from the main roads on the border of Võru and Valga Counties. It was originally set up to protect the characteristic rolling landscape with numerous lakes between wooded hillocks and to preserve the local dispersed settlement pattern. Karula has not yet been discovered by mass tourism and the local people mainly lead simple and traditional lives. One of the actual aims of the National Park is to create conditions making the people wish to remain in the country and to continue their traditional work in the fields and forests. There are nature trails for the visitors, on which you will hear numerous local legends, opportunities to taste farm food and undergo folk medicine practices. The modern visitor centre at Lake Ähijärv has an age-old smoke sauna right on the lake shore reminding one of Karula's main value – the opportunity of transporting yourself to the past.

Hilly landscape near Kaika ▽

◁ Observation tower
on Suur-Munamägi

View from Suur-Munamägi △

Haanja

The highest point in Estonia, **Suur-Munamägi** (Big Egg Hill, 318 meters above sea level) logically lies in the country's loftiest upland, Haanja. The view from the Munamägi tower, built in 1939, makes every Estonian's heart swell – it is the highest point in the Baltic countries, and in a clear weather you can see the spires of Tartu, 70 kilometres away. The winding shorelines of Lake Vaskna and Lake Tuuljärv and the county seat of Võru are clearly in view. The view from the tower has gradually become more and more forested. The age-old spruces have been growing in stoic peace, compelling the people to build the tower higher from time to time. A memorial tablet on its wall is dedicated to the first Estonian to have reached the peak of Mount Everest, 30 times as high as Munamägi. He was Alar Sikk, a man born in these parts, and he made the conquest in 2003.

Looking directly north from Munamägi in the direction of Võru you cannot help noticing another hill. It is Vällamägi, the second highest summit in Estonia (304 meters), but the loftiest in Estonia in terms of relative height – 88 metres. There is a sign-posted nature trail leading across Vällamägi.

The terrain in Haanja rises above 250 meters above sea level in quite an extensive area. The uplands were formed at a place where the continental ice stopped longer than elsewhere. As a result the sheet of ice left a lot of moraine when it melted down and numerous lakes, a total of more than 300, were formed instead. In the spring snow melts later in Haanja than elsewhere in Estonia – when children in Tallinn already admire the first spring flowers, skiing lessons can still be held at the Haanja sports school.

The scenic rolling landscape with the long and deep **Rõuge Primeval Valley** where seven lakes lie at close quarters from each other is situated at the north-western edge of the Haanja Upland. The biggest of the seven is Lake Rõuge

Suurjärv, (the Big Lake of Rõuge), which is also the deepest in Estonia, reaching down up to 38 metres. Several side valleys fork out into the rims of the Rõuge primeval valley, the best known of them being Ööbiku-org (Nightingale Valley), named so after the nightingales singing there in the spring.

A tourist information centre is open on a bank of Rõuge Suurjärv, which is also the starting point of several nature trails for walkers and cyclists.

Taevaskoja

The primeval valley of the Ahja River offers the experience of genuine primordial nature. The bank of the river rises up to 38 meters from the valley floor, featuring magnificent Old Red Devonian sandstone outcrops of which those of Suur-Taevaskoda and Väike-Taevaskoda are known the

▽ **Suur-Taevaskoja sandstone outcrop on the Ahja River**

best. The name Taevaskoda (Heavenly Hall) apparently refers to a sacred place of prehistoric Estonians.

The surrounding forest is about 150 years old and criss-crossed with foot and riding paths.

Carved into the rock wall of Väike-Taevaskoda is Neitsikoobas (Virgin's Cave) and close to it Emaläte (Mother Spring) with reportedly health-bringing water.

There are numerous legends connected with the Ahja River. Their characters are mostly fugitives looking for refuge from war, imprisoned virgins or the Old Heathen. Naturally also underground castles and secret passages feature in the stories.

A few kilometres north of Taevaskoja lies the **Akste Ant Country**. Visits to this 193-hectare nature reserve are strictly in the company of a guide. On the tour through the woods the visitor will get an overview of red wood ants' life and see their piles, some of which are up to 2 metres high.

Karilatsi, a place about a dozen kilometres from Taevaskoja has the Põlva Farm Museum, an open air museum on five hectares where one gets a thorough overview of the local peasants' life in former times.

◁ **Giant anthill**
in the Akste Ant Kingdom

Seto Country

The historical Seto Country lies in the far southeastern corner of Estonia. The main interest in the area is ethnographic as it has been influenced by both Russian and Estonian culture. By their origin the Seto are descendants of Estonians, who have lived in close contact with Russians for long centuries. Seto Country was part of Russia since the 14th century and the Seto are Orthodox, with clear Russian influences in their language, traditions and style of houses.

From the War of Independence until World War II the Seto Country formed the Petseri County within Estonia. In 1944 the Soviet Union moved the administrative border between its then administrative units, the Russian Soviet Federative Soviet Republic and the Estonian SSR, assigning two thirds of the former Petseri County, including the county seat of Petseri, to Russia. The latter is famous for its monastery, whose golden cupolas can be seen across the border in Russia, but the Soviet administrative border is now the factual national border and it is impossible to get there without crossing it. There are four Seto rural municipalities in Estonia, and Seto farm museums in Obinitsa and Saatse. A strict border regime since 1991 has made it difficult to maintain contacts between the Seto in Estonia and in Russia. Family relations have been interrupted and the Seto keep moving away from the

Russian side of the border. However, only recently there was an Estonian school operating in Petseri providing education to children of the Seto.

If a hundred years ago the total number of the Seto was 17,000 then today it is believed there are just a few thousand of them. There are considerably more people with Seto roots and those respecting Seto culture.

There has been a kind of rebirth of the Seto in the recent years – people have become proud of their Seto roots and keep alive their old customs.

For example on Orthodox religious festivals families have the habit of going to the cemetery where they lay food and drink on their lost relatives' graves and so are together with the deceased during the meal. Seto folk songs, performed mostly by women, are unique in style. They are based on improvisations and their subject matter is daily life. They are performed by a lead singer and a chorus when everyone joins in.

The folk costumes of Seto women are beautifully decorated, with a huge brooch on the breast adorned with silver coins from the Russian imperial period. Legends about a Seto king go back to a very distant past, but Days of the Seto Kingdom are held every year. A substitute of the king is then elected with credentials to conduct the business of the Seto during the next year.

Seto Country is very beautiful for its nature. There are dry pinewoods alternating with flat hills, as well as many narrow steep-sloped valleys. Unfortunately a lot of the land lies fallow — the number of population has declined by one third in the Seto Country over the past fifteen years.

Seto Farm Museum

△ **Värska Sanatorium**

Värska

One of the historical centres in the Seto Country is **Värska**. The area stands out for its dry pinewoods, sandy heaths and general abundance of edible mushrooms and berries. Värska Bay, widening out into Lake Peipsi is actually a flooded river mouth where large curative mud deposits have been discovered. The ground in the vicinity of Värska contains mineral water that is directly bottled as it mergers from the borehole. The saltier mineral water, like also the lake mud, is used for immersion therapy at the local rehabilitation centre. Thanks to the mineral water, curative mud, dry air and ozone-rich pinewoods Värska has grown into a pleasant resort in the recent decades.

The head of Värska Bay is the location of the Seto Farm Museum, where it is possible to see the typical closed inner yard of Seto farms. The museum is full of life – various concerts are held and handicraft courses are organised there and it is possible to order festive meals of traditional local food.

▽ **Ruins of the Vastseliina Order Castle**

Piusa River Primeval Valley

The Piusa has one of the steepest gradients among Estonian rivers; in places it is a match even to rough mountain streams. For long centuries the middle reaches of the Piusa constituted the border between the lands of the Order and of Russia. Later it was the borderline between Petseri and Võru Counties. In the 14th century the powerful **Vastseliina Castle**, the easternmost outpost of Old Livonia, was erected on a steep promontory overlooking a river bend white with rapids. The nearest Russian castle was situated at Izborsk some thirty-five kilometres to the east. The cannon of the Vastseliina Castle had unique decorations. In the Middle Ages the chapel of the Vasteliina Castle was known as a destination of pilgrimages from all over Europe. The holy cross kept there granted indulgence from sins for forty days, as confirmed by Pope Innocent VI in 1354. The Vastseliina Castle and the settlement around it were destroyed by the Russians in the Great Northern War. Today some stretches of wall and a couple of cannon towers survive of the castle, and conservation of its ruins is underway.

The Piusa is remarkable for numerous Devonian sandstone outcrops in the stretch of the river between Vastseliina and Tamme. Locally the sandstone outcrops are often called walls and there are about a dozen of them in number. The Piusa walls give the primeval valley a real dimension of eternity. The age of the whitish yellow sandstone walls, with lichens growing here and there on the rocks, amounts to 400 million years. The highest of the walls – that of Suur-Härma, rises up to 43 meters above the surface of the river. Old watermills can often be seen in the stretches of the river where the gradient is the steepest. Once there were more than thirty of them on there, but only of few may be in operation today.

The **Piusa sandstone caves** is a unique site – kilometres upon kilometres of mighty labyrinths created as a result of glass sand extraction in the years 1922–66. Today it supports one of the biggest bat colonies in Eastern Europe. The former mine passages are not reinforced, therefore it is certainly necessary to have a guide on a visit to the labyrinths. An information point of the caves provides information on the history and geology of the Piusa sand quarry.

◁ **High bank of the Piusa**
◁ **Piusa**
◁ **Entrance to the Piusa sandstone caves**
◁ **Old watermill on the Piusa**

The Härma Wall rising to 45 meters above the Piusa River